Beginner English Grammar Guide for English as a Second Language Students

MerriLee Leonard

Kendall Hunt
publishing company

Cover image © Shutterstock.com

Kendall Hunt
publishing company

www.kendallhunt.com
Send all inquiries to:
4050 Westmark Drive
Dubuque, IA 52004-1840

Copyright © 2018 by Kendall Hunt Publishing Company

ISBN: 978-1-5249-6270-8

All rights reserved. No part of this publication may be reproduced, stored in a retrieval system, or transmitted, in any form or by any means, electronic, mechanical, photocopying, recording, or otherwise, without the prior written permission of the copyright owner.

Published in the United States of America

Contents

Letter to English as a Second Language (ESL) Teachers   v

A Word from the Author   vii

Lesson 1	1
Lesson 2	9
Lesson 3	13
Lesson 4	17
Lesson 5	21
Lesson 6	25
Lesson 7	29
Lesson 8	33
Lesson 9	35
Lesson 10	41

Lesson Review   49

Appendix: Answer Keys   59

Word Lists   65

Letter to English as a Second Language (ESL) Teachers

This beginner ESL grammar book is specially designed for non-native English speakers with very little knowledge of English grammar. If you should elect to use this book in your classroom as a stand-alone for a grammar class, know that you can guide your students step-by-step by explaining each lesson to them. As you introduce each new concept, it might be helpful to see vivid illustrations on the chalkboard to support each lesson. For comprehension purposes, I would suggest students participate fully with you—during lecture and with your proactive instruction showing illustrative examples on the chalkboard or an overhead presentation to help students grasp difficult rules they might find too challenging. To ensure your students fully understand your lesson, repeating parts of the lesson you believe students are having difficulty with is recommended. The reflective teaching approach in combination with the question-and-answer (Q&A) instruction format—should be a useful method for reinforcement.

Because ESL students can be easily confused by grammar rules—there are multitudes of them—I highly recommend repeating or reteaching basic concepts. This book is written to minimize those excessive rules for the main purpose of easy application, understanding and memory retention. Teaching ESL students the basic rules—piece-by-piece instead of in one huge bite—is key to their learning the foundation of this material. Handouts are always a good backup for every lesson review with your students. Handouts are advantageous during class hours and for study at home—for further understanding of the materials and as a reference guide.

To conclude, you will find that there are fewer pages in this grammar book compared to a grammar book designed for professional writers. In addition to fewer lessons, this book for beginning English learners contains many exercises that you can give to your students for practice—during class hours and for at-home assignments. All fill-in-the-blank short quizzes have answer keys provided in the appendix for your students to check their answers. I have also included a minidictionary for the meanings of confusing words. Please take time to peruse through pages. Enjoy teaching your students with this book. Thank you.

MerriLee Leonard
M.A.Ed.,TESL
ACLI: Lecturer
NOVA Workforce
Northern Virginia Community College

A Word from the Author

Why is it important to learn English grammar rules? The short answer to this question is, because the English language has rules that must be followed to communicate [talking] and to write well. In other words, because English grammar rules provide a systematic process for the English language to be understood. The grammar rules in English are organized by **tense** or **tenses**—to take one example. In your own language, are there rules that must be used as a guide to learn that language? The English language also has a system that you must learn to be understood—especially when you are talking with another person who is a native English speaker but also for grammatically correct writing composition.

To my ESL English learners, this book is carefully put together for you. You were my inspiration when I meticulously gathered all the learning materials together in this starter grammar book for English as a second language (ESL) students worldwide. The language in this book is purposefully chosen so that you can understand each lesson very easily. You can take this book with you to your ESL classes, or take it while visiting your friends and family members. Share this book with those you know who have long desired to learn English but gave up at some point—for whatever reason or circumstance. In this book, you will have plenty of opportunity to practice what you have learned. As you *plug* and *chug* with each lesson, be mindful of what *tense* you are working on or studying.

I have been very careful to make sure the materials in this book will not only help you learn basic grammar but to also help you polish your speaking power. *Students must be willing to put in the effort—to work hard—to achieve the goal they have set for themselves and ultimately to succeed.* In other words, in this case, believe that you can learn English and you are intelligent enough to speak it fluently! This book will take you far and high as you motivate yourself to achieve English proficiency. The secret to success in learning a new language is patience—it's a progression over time. Be patient with yourself and learn to pace your learning.

Study when you know you are most alert. If you are most alert at night and will learn better at night, then study this book at night. On the other hand, if you are a midday learner and could retain new information best at that time, then study at midday. Some learners prefer to study alone in quiet surroundings; others prefer to study outdoors. Pick the environment or setting where you will concentrate the best as you study. It's important to study in a peaceful location so that you can concentrate better and your mind can record what you have learned.

One last suggestion: I would highly recommend that you find a small study group you feel comfortable studying with. I like the idea of having the opportunity to discuss your knowledge with others, people who are in the same situation as you. If you are this type of a learner, go ahead and join a small study group. Express your thoughts and feelings about the improvements or difficulties you are experiencing with your study group members—don't be shy! Ask questions!

I have provided you with everything that you need to succeed and understand the basic rules of English grammar. You will find answers to every practice (open-book) short quiz and exercise in the back of the book. You will learn the foundation of writing by learning to write short sentences as a beginner in the English language. If you feel confused and don't understand the rules after your first reading, go back and read them again and again—until you get it!

Before we begin, I need you to look at the Appendix at the back of the book to see the answer keys to all your practice exercises at the end of every lesson. Another part I want you to see is the list of verbs on pages 66–75. You will need these pages as you go along (plug and chug) with your lessons to be sure you have the correct answers to the fill-in-the-blank practice questions. Happy trails!

Mental Notes

- English grammar has plenty of rules.
- Learn the process of elimination.
- You can learn.
- Take deep breaths right now.
- Have a clear mind.
- Be ready to learn.
- Concentrate on learning the verb tenses.
- The subject must agree with the correct verb tense.
- Your sentence is about the subject *not* the verb.
- Have a notebook and a pen ready for note taking.
- Nouns will be a part of your study but not in great details.
- Noun information is on page 76.
- You will learn grammar in less time than you think.
- Do not rush to learn; take all the time you need until you get it.
- Take breaks and drink a glass of water.
- Think deeply about the lesson you are studying.

Now let's start our first lesson!

Lesson 1

There are Five Types of Tenses

1. Present Tense

2. Past Tense

3. Future Tense

4. Past Participle: Past Participle Tense

5. Progressive Tense: Continuous Tense

Because the goal of this beginner grammar book is for you to learn the rules with little mental stress and in less time than normal, we will study all five tenses by minimizing the excessive difficult rules of English grammar. Follow every lesson carefully and take as much time as you need—to really understand the correct rules.

Let's start with subject and verb agreement.

Subject and Verb Agreement: The Backbone of English Grammar
The basic rule of a correct English sentence: A sentence must have a subject and a verb—basic sentence.

Example: **I** play; **She** sings; **He** writes; **You** cook; **We** travel; **They** work; **It** walks, and so on. All of these examples are in the *present tense*.

Reality check: Speaking and writing [communication] have the same rules in the English language.

    Ask yourself: Where is the subject?
    Ask yourself: Where is the verb?
    Ask yourself: Is my tense correct?
    Subjects: |I|; |she|; |he|; |you|; |it| = singular [one single thing]
    Subjects: |you|; |we|; |they| = plural [more than one]

The verbs: |play|; |sings|; |writes|; |cook|; |travel|; |work|; |walks|

The subjects: |I|; |she|; |he|; |you|; |we|; |they|; |it|

For longer sentences, you will find more than one subject and verb, and they are usually right *next to each other*. Closely observe the examples below.

The following sentence examples are in the *past tense*, NOT *present tense*, with **-ed** verbs.

Example: I stay**ed** up all night, clean**ed** all night, and work**ed** all night. The verbs are: stay**ed**, clean**ed**, and work**ed**. The subject is the person who is doing the action or the person who is talking in the sentence.

Explanation: The subject |I| is the person who stay*ed* up all night, clean*ed* all night, and work*ed* all night. |I| is our subject in that sentence. The **-ed** ending attached to the base verb tells us that each event happened in the past—it's over and finished. You will talk this way and write this way.

Another example: They walk**ed**, talk**ed**, and play**ed** soccer at the park yesterday. The verbs are: walk*ed*, talk*ed*, and play*ed*. The subject is: [They] because |they| are the people who played soccer at the park yesterday. The sentence is all about the subject |they|. It's telling us what the subject |they| did at the park *yesterday*—past tense.

Past tense example: The ball flew out of the park at the game last night. The subject in this sentence is the |ball| and the verb is |flew|. This sentence is written in the *past tense*. Your hint that it is in the past tense is *last night*—the sport or the game ended last night.

Remember: A complete sentence must have a *subject* and a *verb*, and they must agree with a correct tense to be correct! Do not always look for a first person as a subject; any object can be a subject, also. Ask yourself, *What is being talked about in the sentence? Who is doing the talking in the sentence?* |He|; |she|; and |it| are just three examples that can be subjects in a sentence, but they are not always. See the table on page 57 for subject examples.

Question: What is the correct English sentence?

Answer: Subject + correct verb tense + what you want to say or write about the subject—not about the verb. The verb must agree with what you are talking about. Are you talking about present event, past event, future event?

The other definition of a correct sentence in English is: Subject + verb + noun or object.

Read the example sentence:

Example: I have a new cell phone. The subject is = |I| and the verb is = |have|. In that sentence, the person is saying that he or she has a new cell phone—the sentence is about the subject |I|— the subject |I| is doing the talking in that sentence. The *cell phone* is the = object or a noun. Do you see the point? If not yet, don't worry—there are more detailed explanations in this book.

Mental Notes

- A sentence must have a subject + correct verb + what you want to report or say about the subject.
- When you talk or write, be sure your subject and verb agree in tense.

- Practice your English by speaking English with someone every day.
- Practice pronouncing English words you find difficult to pronounce before going to bed.
- Correct pronunciation of any word is important in English communication.

Now let's learn a little more about the subject of a sentence.

What is a Subject?

Let's find the *subject* in the sentence. First, ask yourself [again] where is the subject in the sentence? You could also ask: Who is the subject in the sentence?

Answer: The *subject* in the sentence is the person or thing being talked about or the person doing the talking in the sentence—it can be: |I|; |You|; |He|; |She|; |It|; |They|; |We|; or any object |ball|; |bicycle|; |book|; |eyeglasses|; and so on.

Sentence Examples: I want to learn English. In this simple sentence, [I] is the one who is talking in the sentence because [I] is the one who wants to learn English. [I] is the subject in this complete and correct sentence—[I] is doing the talking in the sentence. The verb is |want|.

Example of |it or things| as a subject: The eyeglasses |are| broken. |Eyeglasses| is the subject and |are| is the verb. The word *broken* tells us the eyeglasses cannot be used anymore. The sentence is describing the condition of the eyeglasses—broken. The verb |are| is correct because eyeglasses are in the plural form. But if the sentence is describing a single glass, you will have to use a singular verb |is|. We have two eyes, so the glasses must be plural |are|. The subject (glasses) are broken in the present tense condition not in the past. The |eyeglasses| as a subject can also be an |it or a thing| in a complete sentence.

Another Example: The table is long and *it* has plenty of good food. The subject is |table| and the sentence is describing the |table (it)| has plenty of good food. The "it" in the sentence is the "table." And because "table" is a single item, your verb must be |is| not |are|. This sentence is also in the present tense not past.

Mental Notes

- The writer of the sentences [above] is reporting the condition of the subject NOT the condition of the verb.
- You will also write this way in English—write or report about the subject only, NOT about the verb in your sentence.
- Report or write what the subject is about in your sentence.
- Be sure your verb tense agrees with the subject.
- Verb tense must be in correct agreement with what you are talking about or writing.

What is a Fully Complete English Sentence?

Answer: Subject + correct verb tense + your report or description about the subject. The subject (only) takes the lead of your complete sentence, not the verb. In short, you will be writing or describing about the subject only in your sentence! *Verbs* have different tenses—be sure your subject is paired correctly with the right verb tense.

Remember, the English grammar rules are the same when you talk with a native English speaker and when you write in English.

Explanation of subject: If you are talking about yourself, for example, and you want to write down what you are saying, you would be the subject of that sentence you are writing down.

Example: I want to finish college, find a good paying job, and then get married. In that sentence |first person (I)| is the subject of the sentence—who is talking: before I marry, I want to first finish college, get a good paying job, and then get married. I am reporting about myself in that sentence. You will talk or write about other people or friends this way—reporting or explaining what you and others are telling you. The subject in your sentence is the person you are reporting or talking about.

Example of reporting about the subject: Fernando bought a new red car last week. In this sentence, the subject is |Fernando|. The speaker or the writer in that sentence is reporting or explaining that the subject |Fernando| bought a red car last week. The subject in this sentence dominates the entire sentence. This is the way you will write correctly in complete sentences in English. Remember, your subject must have the right verb tense.

Example: I *was* on the farm *last summer* visiting my aunt Dede and her family.

Explanation: The subject is |I| and the verb is |was|. The rest of the reported words is about what the (subject |I|) is doing last summer. The subject is singular |I| and because the subject must agree with the right verb to be correct, we have to use |was|; it cannot be |were (plural)|. Everything in your sentence must be written out in the past tense because the subject |I| is reporting about visiting aunt Dede and her family *last summer*—in the past. This is the way you will talk and communicate in English—with correct grammar rules.

More Examples

1. Ferdinand Magellan was a Portuguese world explorer who claimed the Philippines in 1521 for the King and Queen of Spain.

   The subject in this sentence is |Ferdinand Magellan| and the verb is |claimed|. The verb must be in the past tense with **-ed** ending because Magellan claimed the Philippines in the year 1521—past.

2. The tall tree is being chopped up by loggers.

   Again, the subject in this sentence is the |tree| and the verb is |is|. The subject |tree| is an |object| and another name for it is a |noun|. The sentence is in the **present tense**.

3. My grandfather enjoys sitting in his rocking chair before going to bed.

   The subject is: |grandfather| and the verb is: |enjoys sitting|. The sentence is in the **present** because of the verb "enjoys sitting" without adding -ed on the verb ending.

4. The sombrero hat was blown away by a strong wind.

   The subject is the object |sombrero hat| and the verb is |was blown|. The sombrero is an object and it is the same as a noun. The sentence is in the **past** because of the verb "was."

5. My classmate Nguyen from Vietnam wanted to become an airplane pilot.

   This sentence is in the **past tense** because of the verb "wanted." The subject is "Nguyen."

Mental Notes

- The subject |it| in the sentence can be anything (wild card).
- It is a wild card because you have to figure out what the |it| in the sentence is.
- A subject |it| in the sentence is the same as an object or a noun.
- A subject is often right next to the verb.
- If you are going to talk or write about a single person or an item, your verb must also be singular |is|. But if your subject is talking about more than one persons or items, then your verb must be |are|.

Now let's go chug for the "verb."

What is the Verb in the Sentence?

The verb is the *life* or the *engine* of every sentence—because the verb can stand alone and still be understood!

Examples: Talk, cry, sing, smile, dance, stop, yield, go, bathe, walk, and so forth. You can tell someone anyone of these words and they'll understand what you are saying to them. But because we would normally communicate not just with a single word but rather in a conversational mode, we have to learn the rules of English grammar to speak and write English correctly.

Let's Practice Together

Lesson One Practice

Direction: Find the subject and the verb. Check your answers in the appendix.

1. The birds are singing on the tree.

   Find the subject and the verb in this short sentence.

2. I hope to go to college when I am done high school.

Find the subject and the verb. Did you check your answers in the appendix?

Mental Notes

- Who is the subject again in this example?
- What is the subject again?
- The writer is reporting about the subject, not about the verb.
- The verb must agree with the subject.
- The verb must agree with the tense.

Now let's go find the verb in the sentence.

What is a Verb?

Answer: A verb is the word in the sentence that is doing the action or the action the subject is doing in the sentence.

Example: I want to learn English. The verb in this complete and correct sentence is |want|. Why is |want| the verb? Ask yourself, what is the subject doing in the sentence? Answer: |I (subject)| want to learn English—|want| is doing the action in this sentence; |want (verb)| is the verb. I want to learn English = is a complete sentence with correct subject and verb agreement.

Another Example

He was dancing to modern rhythm. Who is the subject in this sentence?

Ask yourself: Where is the verb that does the action in that sentence? What is the subject |he| doing?

- Who is the verb again in this example?
- What is the verb again?
- The subject must agree with the verb to be correct.
- In what tense is the subject talking?

Mental Note

A correct and complete sentence in English must have a subject + verb + your report about the subject—the remaining words in your sentence are called predicate. We will go over *predicate* in more details in Lesson Two. You need to understand who or what is the subject first, so that your verb is in correct agreement with the subject. Watch out for tense—it must have the right verb!

Example: I bought a new bicycle today. |I (subject)|; |bought (verb)| a new bicycle = object (the same as a noun). The tense is in the past = bought.

Explanation: The subject above is telling you and I that he or she bought a new bicycle. Notice that the entire sentence is talking about what the subject bought—the bicycle. If you look at the "tense," the subject is telling us that he or she bought the new bicycle today—in the present tense. The subject |I| is saying he or she already bought the bicycle today. The buying activity is finished, even though the subject |I| just bought the bicycle today. The subject is saying that he or she already paid for the new bicycle. This is why you need to pay close attention to the verb—because the verb will tell you if the action is happening in the present, past, or future tense.

Here are examples about activity that we do "right now" or "today." The verb tense is present tense because the action is happening in the present.

1. I go to school today.

2. I am in school today.

3. We are at the cinema today.

4. He is playing basketball today.

5. My father goes to work today.

6. My mother goes to the market today.

7. She has plenty of food in her lunch box.

Explanation: There are 24 hours in one day. Think of things that you do and accomplish in the 24-hour time span (one day). Go back to the *bicycle* example above and read again. Even though the buying of the bicycle happened today, the verb "bought" is correct—because the subject |I| already bought and paid for his new bicycle within the 24-hour period of time. Notice that the verb is in the past tense—because the activity [buying a new bicycle] the subject did is done and finished.

Examples: All sentence examples are in the present tense—right now.

1. I am having dinner with my family *right now*.

2. I am doing my homework *right now*.

3. I am shopping with my mother *right now* at the mall.

4. I am studying Lesson Two in my grammar book *right now*.

5. My father is walking our dog *right now* at the park.

Explanation: All sentence examples are happening within the period 24-hour time span. That means "right now" is within the 24-hour time line = 1 day. Your "verb" in your sentence and talking [English communication] should be in complete agreement with what you are trying to say—including what you did today.

Example: My friend Antonio told me his parents will send him to the United States to study medicine when we are finish senior high school.

Question: What is the subject reporting in that sentence? Who is the subject? Does the verb agree with the subject? How about the tense?

Answer: The subject is talking about his friend Antonio and is reporting about where Antonio's parents will send him to study medicine. The verb agrees with the subject |told (past tense)| because Antonio already told his friend where his parents will send him to school. The second verb |will| is in the future tense—because the subject (the person who is talking in the sentence) is reporting that Antonio is not done high school yet, but when Antonio is finished high school, his parents will send him to the United States to study medicine. Notice that the entire sentence is reporting NOT about the verb but about the subject only—Antonio. You will write and talk this way also.

Lesson One Exercise One

Now, let's do a short practice together.
Find the subject and verb and circle them in the following sentences. Check your answers in the appendix.

1. The groom is handsome.

2. Lucinda looks beautiful in her bride gown.

3. The bridesmaids are attractive.

4. The ring bearer is a boy.

5. The flower girl is pretty in pink.

Lesson 2

Now, let's talk about the *heart* of the English language—the verb tense or tenses are closely linked to time. The tense in your sentence tells whether you are talking about something that is happening in the |present time|, |future time|, or |past time|. Each one of the tenses has its own unique rule that you need to pay close attention to—so that your talking [communication] is right and your English is written correctly.

- Before we move on, you need to remember that in the United States, grammar rules are called:

    Present Tense, Past Tense, Future Tense, Past Participle Tense, and Progressive Tense.

    For the sake of simplification, we will take out the word |perfect| from all three tenses. This book is written for beginner grammar learners. The word *perfect* simply means ongoing action in that particular tense.

- It is not important for you to know the word *perfect* just yet. Pay attention to the tense or tenses—because your verb tense in the sentence must agree with the subject to be correct! All tenses are already labelled correctly without the word *perfect*.

Read the following carefully and see what happens to the verb as you change the *tense* in each sentence. Pretend you are the person talking in all three sentences.

Example: You are the speaker [the person who is talking] in all three sentences. This sentence is in the conversational style.

1. My parents *want* me to become a doctor when I go to college.

2. I *told* them I will give it a try.

3. My parents *were* happy when they *heard* me say I will give it a try.

Explanation: Sentence one is in the present tense with the verb |want| not |wanted|. Sentence two is written in the past tense |verb (told)| not |tell|, and sentence three also in the past tense |verbs (were and heard)|. The rest of the information in all three sentences is reporting about the comments of the speaker's parents. Go back and read the rules again if you didn't understand yet.

Mental Notes

- What are tenses that must agree with my correct sentence?
- Is my sentence singular or plural?
- Does my subject agree with the verb tense?
- My sentence should be about the subject NOT about the verb.

Now let's go plug and chug down to verb tense rules.

Let's go learn the "tenses."

Sentence Sequence Examples

Present Tense: I am *taking* an English class this semester (You are in this class right now—present tense).

Past Tense: I *took* an English class last semester (You are finished with this class—past tense).

Future Tense: I *will* take an English class next semester [You are planning to register for an English class in the future time—future tense].

Participle Tense: I *have gone* to college with my high school friend—|Have| + participle verb |gone|.

Questions:

- Where is the verb in the sentence?
- Why did the base verb [**take**] change in each sentence?
- How did it change?
- The verb and tense must agree with what you are talking about so that the person you are talking to will understand what you are saying.

Lesson Two Practice

Direction: Find the verbs in all three examples and you will find out why.
Think this way: Verb and tense rules.

Table 2.1 is showing you and me that the verb must agree with the corresponding tense.

Now, let's test your understanding. Find the subject and the verb and circle them. I want you to write down: Present, past, or future tense for each sentence. Check your answers in the appendix.

Table 2.1

Present Tense	Past Tense	Past Participle
Choose	Chose	Chosen

Correct sentence examples:

1. I *choose* to buy a new backpack *this semester* = Present Tense

2. I *will choose* to buy a new backpack *next summer* = Future Tense

3. I *chose* to buy a new backpack *last month* = Past Tense

4. I *had chosen* to buy a new backpack *last year* = Past Participle

Mental Notes

- Notice the verb |choose| is the same in the present and future tenses. The verb |choose| is also a base verb.
- All lessons in this book will cover all three tenses.
- Focus on learning the tense or tenses so that your verb is right.
- Is your sentence talking about today, tomorrow, or yesterday?
- Read the sentence below to learn about the predicate.

Let's Understand "Predicate."

What is a Predicate?

Predicate example:

Sentence: My favorite subjects in high school are math, social studies, and English.

Direction: Underline the subject in that sentence and circle the verb. The subject is |math, social studies, and English| and the verb is |are|. The rest of the sentence is the predicate.

Question: What do you think is wrong with each sentence below? Can you correct them?
Sentence one: I go to see my friend two days ago.

Sentence two: Lisa is here last night.

Sentence three: I buy it from the store last month.

Question: What's wrong with the verbs? Did you correct all three sentences?

Lesson Two Exercise One

Now let's give your knowledge power a test run to see how much you already understand in this lesson. Check your answers in the appendix. Use the list of verbs on pages 66–75 if you need more help. If you need more time to understand the idea, feel free to go back and read the part you do not understand again.

Direction: Circle the correct subject-verb agreement. What tense do you think each sentence is? Check your answer in the appendix.

1. I see clouds in the sky today.

2. I saw clouds in the sky yesterday.

3. I had seen clouds in the sky last night.

4. She will grow vegetables this spring.

5. He grew vegetables last year.

6. They have grown vegetables before.

7. We like to grow green beans in the springtime.

8. It grows taller than me.

9. My sister is going to college next year.

10. We like to listen to modern music.

Lesson 3

Another verb tense that you must learn is the progressive tense. Progressive tense describes continuous action. Continuous can mean the things we do all the time or things we do normally every day.

Correct examples:

1. I go to the store all the time to buy milk.

2. She washes dishes every day.

3. He goes to work every day.

4. It brings strong winds every fall season.

5. We go to school all year long.

6. My mother drives my sister to school Monday through Friday.

7. My father takes me out to the park on weekends to play soccer.

These are just a few examples of activities we would do regularly or of events observed in our weather every year.

Now let's learn another grammar rule.

The progressive tense can be applied to all tenses: present, future, past tense, and past participle.

Mental Note

The *progressive verbs* are the easiest verbs to remember among all the other tenses in English grammar. All you have to do is add: **-ing** to the ending of the base verb—the present tense verb is the base verb. See the list of base verbs on page 66.

Let's learn the rule of progressive tense now.

Progressive tense rule: All you need to do is add **-ing** to the base verb. The base verb is the **present tense** verb. It doesn't matter whether you are talking about the present, past, future, or progressive tense—the rule stays the same.

Mental Note

In the progressive tense verb: The **-ing** form ending of the verb in your sentence cannot be a verb. The **-ing** verb must be: |am|, |is|, |are|, |was|, |were|, and |been| before the **-ing** form can be considered a correct verb of a sentence.

You have to remember the six (6) *to be* verbs listed above in the progressive tense—you need to memorize them.

Read the example sentences below.

Correct sentence: Tourists have been visit**ing** Disney World since the park opened in October 1971.

    Subject = Tourists
    Verb = been visit**ing**
    Wrong verb = visiting

Make sure your verb agrees with the progressive tense.

Let's examine the verb *to go*.

The base verb is |go| in Table 3.1.

Table 3.1

Progressive Tense or Continuous	Sentence Examples
Present tense	I'm go**ing** to school today |go verb|
Future tense	I will be go**ing** to school tomorrow.
Past tense	I was go**ing** to school yesterday, but I couldn't go because it was raining hard.

Let's learn what the verb *to go* is all about and what happens to the word *go* in the progressive tense rule. Study the rules in Table 3.1.

Table 3.1 shows you that a base verb must stay the same, but you have to add **-ing** to the base verb in all three tenses.

Example of base verb: |run| Add **–ing** = running.

Complete sentence: I am run**ning** right now [run].

Other examples:

He is walk**ing** my dog to the park today [walk].
She is eat**ing** ice cream right now [eat].
I was talk**ing** to my friend yesterday [talk].
I will be travel**ing** to Europe with my family this summer [travel].
They were sit**ting** [sit] on the park bench watch**ing** the sunset [watch].
Another example: base verb: sing. Add -**ing** = singing.
Complete sentence: They lare sing**ing**| karaoke [sing].
Another example of a complete sentence: They lare talk**ing**| too loud [talk].

Mental Notes

- Base verb must have -**ing** ending to all tenses in your sentence.
- Some verbs you have to take out letters and replaced with -**ing**.

Study how the verbs change in Table 3.2.

Table 3.2

Base verbs	Progressive tense sentences
Choose	They are choos<u>ing</u> a bigger house.
Become	He is becom<u>ing</u> a better man.
Drive	She was driv<u>ing</u> so fast in the rain.
Rise	The sun is ris<u>ing</u> in the east.
Freeze	It is freez<u>ing</u> in this room.

Lesson Three: Exercise One

Directions: Now, circle the subject-verb agreement in the 10 sentences below. Check your answer in the appendix. Do you know what tense each sentence is in?

1. I am go*ing* to take a class this semester.

2. I am go*ing* to take an English class next semester.

3. I was go*ing* to take an English class last semester.

4. He was runn*ing* in the park when the rain came.

5. He is talk*ing* on the phone right now.

6. She is leav*ing* in just a few minutes.

7. She was leav*ing* the party when the visitors arrived.

8. They are work*ing* too hard today.

9. They were work*ing* too hard to get a promotion all year long.

10. It is jump*ing* high and low.

These sentences are correct in speech [talking] and in writing—they follow the progressive tense rule. Apply these rules to your writing and it should be correct!

Mental Notes

- Be sure the tense or tenses agree with the **-ing** verb.
- Don't forget to change present tense verb to past tense if you are talking about finished or completed activity.
- Your sentence should be about the subject only and not the verb.
- |Two| mangoes |are| plural and |one| mango |is| singular.
- If you are talking about more than one fruit or person, the verb must be plural; if you are talking about one fruit or person or animal or item, the verb must be singular.
- The base verb is the same as the present tense verb.

A Question for You

Are you ready to test how much you already understand?

Write your own sentence examples with **-ing** verb on a separate sheet of paper and see if you understand the rule of adding **-ing** to your base verb. Ask someone you know who can speak English well for help. Be sure to follow the rules you've learned.

Let's move on to lesson four and learn about **was** and **were** verbs.

Lesson 4

Now, let's learn two more verbs: was and were. Refer to Table 4.1.

Table 4.1

Past Tense Singular Verb	was	One person or object
Past Tense Plural Verb	were	Two persons or objects
	Examples	
I was done playing.		They were on vacation.
He was waiting for me.		We were studying.
She was with him at the mall.		The children were singing.

Table 4.1 shows |was (singular verb)| and |were (plural verb)|. Both verbs are in the past tense.

A singular subject in your sentence can be: |I|, |he|, |she|, |it|, a name of a person [Susan or John] or names of persons. |It| can be any type of object.

Plural subjects in your sentence can be: |we| or more than one of an object [balls, apples, shoes, bags, books, tables, shirts, cars, and so on]. Notice, each one of the example has an -s ending |plural|.

Examples
Read and learn

Tense: Past tense

Verbs: was and **were**

1. I *was asked* to run a mile |past tense|.

2. He *was asked* to write a short letter |past tense|.

3. She *was asked* to do a class presentation |past tense|.

17

18 • Beginner English Grammar Guide for English as a Second Language Students

4. It *was asked* of him to obey school rules |past tense|

5. The *tables were* very clean = past tense [plural subject].

6. My *shoes were* dirty = past tense [plural subject].

7. The *soccer ball was* borrowed = past tense [singular subject].

8. *They were* shopping for a new car = past tense [plural subject].

Mental Note

If your "subjects" are:

|I|, |he|, |she|, |it| = was (singular)

|We|, |they|, |you (plural)| = were (plural)

Examples: when the subject is "you."

1. *You are* with me in my English 101 class this semester = present tense (singular).

2. *You were* with me in my English 102 class last year = past tense (singular).

3. *You are* bright students = present tense (plural). The subject |you| means everybody in the class and because the subject is plural, the verb must also be plural |are|.

Question for You

Did you understand the rules? If not, go back and read this part of the chapter again and be sure to do the exercises. Examples and exercises should help you understand the lesson.

Now let's learn about "conditional."

What Is Conditional?

Conditional sentence rule: Study the chart in Table 4.2 carefully.

Special rule for **conditional** with |were| verb.

Rule 1: Use |were| for giving friends advice.

Rule 2: |were| is for first person speaker and must begin with |if|.

Rule 3: |were| is used when talking about present tense event—in most cases, but not always.

- Conditional is something you wish someone would rather do.
- The sentence should start by saying: *If I were you, I would* . . . .

Table 4.2 is about the conditional and shows you how to use the |were| verb in the [present tense] form when the speaker is the first person.

Mental Notes

- You will use conditional in the present tense.
- Singular subject must have singular verb.
- Plural subject must have plural verb.

Table 4.2 Conditional Rule

First-person speaker	Sentence Examples
If I were you . . .	I would take Susie to the dance.
If I were you . . .	I would study hard for the exam.
If I were you . . .	I would finish college.
If I were you . . .	I would travel the world.
If I were Jonah . . .	I would take Nineveh out to dinner.

Practice Exercise One

Plural sentence examples: Now that you have studied the conditional rule, I want you to do your own sentence examples by filling in the blank spaces below. There are seven (7) questions.

1. *We* asked to be seated by the window = past tense with plural subject.

2. *They* asked to be seated by the window = past tense with plural subject.

3. **All** of us asked to be seated by the window = past tense with plural subject.

4. The *cars* and the *horses* **were** crossing on a very busy highway last night = past tense with plural subject in agreement with plural verb |were|.

5. *We* **were** at the lingo dance all night last night = past tense with plural verb.

6. *They* **were** at the mall shopping for furniture yesterday = past tense with plural verb.

7. Lucy and Robert **were** at the cinema last week = past tense with plural verb.

Mental Notes

- |Was| and |were| are two verbs in the past tense.
- Do not use these verbs in sentence written in the present tense.
- Do not use *was* or *were* in your present tense talking or writing.
- *Were* as a verb can be used for conditional talking or writing.
- Conditional talking [communication] has a separate rule.

It's time again to test your knowledge power of the lesson.

Lesson Four Exercise

Directions: Fill in the blanks with the correct verb tense. Check the appendix to see if your answers are correct.

1. They _____ at the supermarket yesterday.

2. She _____ at the concert with me last night.

3. We _____ friends for a very long time.

4. He _____ not a good musician.

5. You _____ being rude to them.

6. It _____ not a bad movie at all.

7. I _____ in the shower when you called.

Question: How do you think you did on all practice tests? How much did you learn? Feel free to go back and read the rules again if you didn't do so well on your first try.

Now, let's move on to Lesson Five!

Lesson 5

Take a deep breath before we begin with present tense rules.

As already explained, the present tense has its own rule and does *not* follow the same grammar rules as the future tense and the past tense.

- Verb must change as you talk—because each tense has its own special rule. The grammar rule holds true as you speak and as you write.

Mental Note

Do not mix present tense, future tense, and past tense in your talking [communication] and writing unless you are reporting or describing a finished activity. The verb must change as you talk [speak] or write—to agree with the correct *tense*.

Present tense rule: For any activity that you are doing right now, in the present, use the present tense verb, which is the same as a base verb. See the list of verbs on pages 66–75.

New Rule: If there is an **-s** to the subject, do not add **-s** to the verb. If you do *not* see an **-s** to the subject sentence, you must add **-s** to the base verb. Look at Table 5.1.

Table 5.1

Present Tense Only	Base Verb	Subject
Sentence Examples	Run, like, fall, care, crave	he, she, it, we, they
He run**s** for a mile.		
She like**s** him very much.		
It fall**s** hard.		
We **care** for you.	Verb does not change	Plural subject
They **crave** water.	Verb does not change	Plural subject

Explanation: The table shows the present tense rule. For the third person singular subject, the verb must have an -s ending, but no -s ending for |we| or |they| (plural subject): The base verb stays the same.

Mental Note

Remember to add -s ending in your speech [talking] and in your writing if you are talking about present tense activity in *third person* singular subject, but no -s ending for plural subjects. The verbs do not change for plural subjects: |we|, |they|.

Now let's plug and chug with this new rule. Let's give your knowledge a test run.

Lesson Five Exercise

Fill in the 10 sentences below and check your answers in the appendix.

1. It _____ at the mall today. [rains]

2. He _____ tomorrow. [leaves]

3. She _____ her boyfriend this weekend. [sees]

4. It _____ of wisdom from days of old. [speaks]

5. The bird _____ in the trees. [sings]

6. We _____ about your future. [care]

7. They _____ English very well. [speak]

8. They _____ on the grass. [walk]

9. She ask _____ for a pencil. [asks]

10. It _____ windy today. [appears]

Examples

I need to call my mother right now to let her know I am working late. The words *right now* means that you want to call your mother *now*. I am in the shower *right now*, so I cannot talk to you. He is watching a TV show *right this minute* and cannot come to the phone. She is washing the dishes *right now*—all sentences are in the present tense.

Read what you have written down aloud with a friend or with a family member. Remember that the sentences you have written down are in the present tense and past tense with **-ing** verbs.

Let's move on to Lesson Six!

Lesson 6

Third person only rule.

Table 6.1 shows the present tense rule in the third person.

Table 6.1

First person: the speaker	The person who is talking
Second person: the person you are talking to	Two people who are talking
Third person: the person or the object you are talking about	Family, friends, the weather
Rule: add -**s**, -**es**, -**ies** to the base verb.	

Explanation: Table 6.1 shows you and me that our communication has three parts:

1. The speaker who is talking

2. The speaker and another person who are talking to each other

3. The topic being talked about

Topic: He, she, it. The third person singular subject in your communication [talking].

    First person: The speaker [the person who is talking].

    Second person: The person you are talking to.

    Third person: The person you are talking about in your talking [communication].

Rule: You need to add -s; -es; -ies to the base verb [only] in your sentence.
See the example sentences below.

Sentence Examples

He, she, it = third person singular subject.

The teacher <u>say</u> to put our assignments on her desk = The teacher <u>says</u> to put our assignments on her desk.

25

The president give an order to obey the law = The president gives an order to obey the law.

1. He sing very well = He sings very well.

2. She visit her mother once a year in San Francisco = She visits her mother once a year in San Francisco.

3. He see his girlfriend on weekends = He sees his girlfriend on weekends.

4. She speak two languages = She speaks two languages.

5. He carry a backpack to school = He carries a backpack to school.

6. The baby cry all day long = The baby cries all day long.

7. It say to donate some of your earnings to good causes = It says to donate some of your earnings to good causes.

8. It shake the floor = It shakes the floor.

9. It use a size A battery = It uses a size A battery.

10. She wear nice jewelry = She wears nice jewelry.

Mental Note

The -s, -es, and -ies rule is only applied in the present tense when talking and in writing. The rule applies to the third person only!

Lesson Six Exercise

Directions: Now practice your knowledge and fill in the blanks below.

1. He like Asian food = He _____ food.

2. He bath every morning = He _____ every morning.

3. He talk too much = He _____ too much.

4. She work in her yard = She _____ her yard.

5. She cut hair = She _____ hair.

6. She clean the house = She _____ the house.

7. He mop the floor = He _____ the floor.

8. She teach English = She _____ English.

9. It seem crooked = It _____ crooked.

10. It appear confusing = It _____ confusing.

11. It fly through the air = It _____ through the air.

12. It smile beautifully = It _____ beautifully.

Directions: Practice all examples aloud with a friend or with a member of your family. Then take out a piece of paper and write as many examples as you can and say them aloud to yourself. Check your answers in the appendix.

Let's chug to **subject–verb agreement** in complete and correct sentences.

If the subject is singular, the verb must also be singular.

If the subject is plural, the verb must also be plural.

Lesson 7

Table 7.1

Verb: *is* and *are*	Examples
is	She *is* bright.
are	We *are* learning English.
is	The book *is* too heavy.
are	The cars *are* new.

Example

Verbs: *are* and *is*

Singular [is]; plural [are].

> One apple or person = singular
>
> Two or more apples or persons = plural

An **apple** a day **is** good for you. Again, you must first find the **subject** and then find the **verb**. The subject *apple* is one = verb must be **[is]** singular.

Apples **are** fruits. Find the subject first to see if it's singular or plural. *Apples* with an **-s** are plural, so the verb must also be plural. For more than one apple, **[are]** is the correct verb.

Sentence: The students are in school.

Find the subject first, and then find the verb to be sure your sentence is correct. The subject is *students*. To follow the given rule of subject-verb agreement—the verb must be **[are]** because *students* [subject] are in the plural form—more than one student. Do not use the verb [is].

Now let's give your knowledge a test drive.

Lesson Seven: Exercise One

Fill in the blanks below and check your answers in the appendix.

1. My shoes _____ black.

2. She _____ tall.

3. He _____ handsome.

4. We _____ smart.

5. They _____ happy.

6. It _____ a basketball game.

7. The papayas _____ yellow.

8. The bread _____ hot.

9. My book _____ green.

10. The chairs _____ high.

More examples:

1. She like**s** to walk in the morning = find the subject first and then find the verb. [She] is the subject and [likes] is the verb. This sentence is in third person singular—present tense rule.

2. That family **is** too quiet = family **is** the subject [singular] and [**is**] is your verb, which is also singular—subject and verb are in correct agreement. A singular subject is required to have a singular verb.

3. The bears, sheep, giraffe, cows, dinosaurs, hippopotamus, and elephants **are** animals you will see in the zoo. The subject in this sentence is more than one: bears, sheep, giraffe, cows, dinosaurs, hippopotamus, and elephants; therefore, your verb must also be plural [**are**] not [is].

Mental Note: If you are talking about one object or thing, do not use the verb [**are**]. If you are talking about more than one object or thing, do not use [**is**]. This is the rule of present tense!

Lesson Seven Exercise Two

Directions: Now it's your turn. Fill-in the blanks below for subject-verb agreement. Choose **are** or **is**. Find the subject first. Check your answers in the appendix.

1. There _____ a pencil on the teacher's desk.

2. She _____ the school principal.

3. He _____ married to a writer.

4. It _____ colored blue, not pink.

5. They _____ professional engineers.

6. There _____ poor people in the world.

7. The houses _____ larger in the suburb than in the city.

- Take out a piece of paper and write your own examples using [is] and [are] verbs. Practice what you wrote down aloud with a friend or with a member of your family with a good command of English.

Let's go to lesson eight!

Lesson 8

In this lesson, you will learn to master writing the base-verb rule and change it into past tense. Look at Table 8.1 to learn the rules.

Table 8.1

Past tense verb **-d**	care = base verb	becomes = care**d**
Past tense verb **-ied**	study = base verb	becomes = stud**ied**

Grammar rule for: -ed and -d

Now let us plug and chug to *past tense rules*:

Rule one: You need to change the base verb from present tense to past tense verb—including the third person present tense.

Rule two: You need to add |**-ed**|, |**-d**|, |**-ied**| to base verb [only] in your sentence.

Rule three: The third person present tense verb must change to a past tense verb.

- You need to memorize the irregular verbs—they have separate rules. I have included a list of irregular verbs for you in this book—see pages 66–70.

Let's go for sentence examples. Pay attention!

1. I ask her a question—present tense.

2. I ask**ed** her a question yesterday—past tense.

3. I talk to her very slowly—present tense.

4. I talk**ed** to her on the phone last night—past tense.

5. He want**s** me just now—present tense.

6. He want**ed** me yesterday—past tense.

7. He walk**s** with his dog—present tense.

8. He walk**ed** with his dog yesterday—past tense.

9. She step**s** on my toe—present tense.

10. She step**ped** on my toe—past tense.

11. She start**s** with a nice introduction—present tense.

12. She start**ed** with a nice introduction—past tense.

13. He lie**s** to me every time we talk—present tense

14. He **lied** to me every time we talked—past tense

Now that you know what to do with the *subject-verb* agreement to create a correct sentence, let's move on to the next lesson.

Lesson 9

This lesson is very important for you to know because it is used in everyday communication [talking]. If you do not yet understand the rules in previous lessons, go back and take all the time you need and review them.

Verb does not change for subjects: **I; you; we; they**. Use base verb only if you are talking about present-tense event or things.

Example:

1. *I* like to read an English book.

2. *You* like ice cream.

3. *We* like to go shopping at the mall

4. *They* like to ride bikes at the park.

The verb changes if you are talking and writing about past-tense topics. You will only change the verb when you talk and in your writing. You can report or talk about any topic you want, but your verb must change – if you are talking about finished (everything) you already did.

Example:

1. I lik**ed** it when my mother used to fix me hot soup when I get sick as a child. = past-tense

2. You said you lik**ed** to play basketball as a young boy. = past-tense

3. We lik**ed** travelling when our children were small and were at home with us. = past-tense

4. They lik**ed** singing and paying guitar in high school. = past-tense

Rule for verb: **Has**

Explanation: The verb |has| is singular and it is also used if a person owns things. You will use |has| for one single subject only as your verb in your talking and in formal writing. Do not use |has| for plural topics or subjects – change your verb to |have| for more than one subject.

Example:

1. Kristina *has* a new car = possession.

2. Jonathan *has* a job at the post office = possession.

3. Jessica *has* a new purse with matching shoes = possession.

4. Scott *has* my backpack = possession.

5. Olivia *has* a dog named Rocky = possession

6. He *has* my keys = possession.

7. She *has* my book = possession.

8. Don *has* his wife's sunglasses = possession.

9. Werusca *has* a lovely daughter. = possession.

10. We *have* a sunny day today = possession.

11. They *have* a large camper = possession.

Let's learn a new verb: **have**.

The verb |have| has a special rule in almost all the tenses you have already learned from previous lessons.

Rules for |have|:

Have is used in sentences about ownership of things you own or things that belong to other people. In other words, it is used when talking about personal property.

What do you see inside your house? Things like refrigerators, desks, lamps, beds, telephones, dinner table, chairs, television, couch, cabinets, clothes, shoes, books, CD player, Nintendo games, and so much more. These are things that belong to you and to other people inside their house. These things are examples of your own personal property or possessions and that of other people.

Have: Can be plural or singular in the sentence.

Have: Must be used in the present tense.

Study Table 9.1 closely.

Table 9.1 Have

Subject	Examples
I	I *have* a girlfriend.
You	You *have* a nice smile.
We	We *have* a new car.
They	They *have* a big house.

The table shows you how to write your simple sentence with the verb |have| verb. All the sentences are in the present tense.

Sentence examples: first person singular

1. I have a high school diploma.

2. I have one sister and one brother.

3. I have one car I really like to drive.

4. I have a good friend.

5. I have nice classmates.

6. I have an intelligent English teacher.

7. I have caring parents I enjoy spending time with.

Present tense: plural subject |have|.

1. We <u>have</u> a good school.

2. We <u>have</u> very warm weather in the summer.

3. We <u>have</u> cats I like to play with at home.

4. They <u>have</u> a nice garden in their backyard.

5. They <u>have</u> a big swimming pool.

6. They <u>have</u> very competent English teachers.

7. They <u>have</u> a karaoke stereo system.

More Examples

Read: You must use the verb |**have**| with the participle verb because this is the rule of English grammar. See Table 9.2 for examples of |**have**| used with participle verbs.

Table 9.2 *Have* with Participle Verbs

Subject	Participle Verb Example
I	I *have lost* my appetite.
you	You *have slept* late this morning.
we	We *have spent* too much money shopping.
they	They *have flown* to Manila before.
we	We *have met* him at the train station.
they	They *have kept* their promise.

The table shows that you have to pair the verb |have| to the participle verb to make your sentence correct. A list of participle verbs is on page 66–70.

Sentence examples:

1. Their sisters **have lost** their keys to their hotel rooms.

2. I **have slept** at my friends' house.

3. We **have left** for work early.

4. They **have arrived** late for school.

Mental Note: |have| is possessive, and |have| can be used by the first person speaker, second person speaker, and the third-person speaker in your talking [communication] and in your writing. Do not forget these *have* rules.

Lesson Nine Exercise

Now that you know the special rules of |have|, take out a piece of paper and write down your answers to the sentences below. Check your answers in the appendix.

1. I _____ a date this evening.

2. I _____ a new car.

3. I don't _____ an English class on weekends.

4. If I can't _____ you, I will stay single.

5. We _____ no electricity right now because of the storm.

6. We _____ not been to Europe, but we hope to go when we have enough money saved.

7. We _____ to go now because I have to do my assignment.

8. We can't _____ recess today because we were not polite to the teacher.

9. They _____ a large family.

10. They _____ to give some of their income to the poor.

11. They wish to _____ a wonderful time at the party tonight.

12. They want to _____ good grades in their English class.

Now let's go plug and chug to the past tense of |have|.

Lesson 10

Study Table 10.1.

Table 10.1 |have| Must Change to |had|

Present Tense = **have**	Past Tense = **had**
Sentence Examples	Sentence Examples
I *have* an English book.	I *had* that English book last semester.
We *have* a dog for a pet.	We *had* a dog for a pet last year.
They *have* a nice garden.	They *had* a nice garden last month.
I *have* a good English teacher.	I *had* a good English teacher last year.

The table shows you the verb |have| used in the present tense and the past tense |had| used in a sentence. These sentences would be correct when you are having a conversation [talking] with another person or you are writing.

Mental Notes

- The past tense of |have| is |had|.
- As you have already learned above, the rules for adding **-ed** and **-d** are necessary in past tense communication [talking] and writing to make your sentences correct.

    Rule 1: |**Had**| is used for a singular subject [I, you, he, she, it] and a plural subject [they, them, we].

    Rule 2: |**Had**| must be used with the past participle form of the verb *to be* in your sentence. You pair them together so that your grammar is correct.

    Rule 3: The verbs |have|, |has|, and |had| must have *participle* verb or **-ed** and **-d** ending for *regular* verbs.

Study Table 10.2 to understand the relationship of the verb |had| and a participle verb.

Table 10.2 Sentence Examples Showing the Relationship of |had| to a Participle Verb

I *had begun* writing my research paper long before it was due.
John *had driven* a car before his parents bought him a new car.
He *had taught* English to adult students last year but not this year.
She *had* already *given* the speech by the time the audience asked to be seated.
They *had seen* Ling-Ling the bear at the zoo before she was taken back to China.
We *had* already *left* Tokyo when the bad storm hit landfall.
My sister *had left* town by the time I got to her apartment.
The wedding *had started* by the time I got to the church.

The table shows you how |**had**| can be used in two separate events in one sentence. One event is over in the past while another event is still happening in the past.

More |**had**| verb examples:

1. I *had told* her to leave early to avoid traffic, but the road was already jammed by the time she left home.

2. He *had sent* her an apology letter, but she was already screaming at me on the phone before the letter arrived.

3. The news *had* already *spread* all over town before it went into print.

4. The rocket ship *had been* to the moon several times before the astronauts found out the radio communication was completely disabled.

5. Miguel *had eaten* the eggs for breakfast before going to school.

Mental Note: Do not use |had| in your talking [communication] or writing if you are talking about present tense events or activities that are not yet finished.

When you have |to| in your sentence, you will need to use the base verb. Remember: [to + verb] in the sentence cannot be considered a correct verb [to buy, to go, to hope, to talk, to run, to sing, to dream, and so forth]. Another one that you need to remember is the word: |be|. You have to use past tense verb after the word |be| in your writing or when you talk.

Sentence examples:

The wild forest is |be| *be*ing clean*ed* by the city council.

The English class schedule is |be| to *be* announc*ed* according to the syllabus.

I have |be| *been* inform*ed* by my mother to take out the dog for a walk.

Kristina said she plans [to buy] a used car. The subject is: Kristina and the verb is [**said**], not *to buy*.

Scott is ordering [to buy] Chinese food at the nearby restaurant. The subject = [**Scott**]; the verb is = [**is ordering**]; not to buy.

Jon had to take a break from working over 5 hours. The subject is = Jon. The verb is = had, not [to take].

More examples: I **had** [to leave] early yesterday for my doctor's appointment. The base verb **leave** must be in the base form—do not change the verb to past tense [left] because of the word |to|. The subject is = [**I**], and the verb is = [**had**].

Lesson Ten: Exercise One

Directions: Now, try answering the questions below with |had + participle| and check your answers on page 62.

1. I had to ask my teacher if I could go to the bathroom.

2. I had to go to the library to return a borrowed book.

3. I had sung my favorite song at the birthday party last night.

4. You *had broken* my heart many times before.

5. You had hidden your true self from me in the past.

6. You had sworn to me, sweetheart, that you will change your wicked ways.

7. Maria had seen the tallest man in the world recorded in the Guinness Book in the Philippines.

8. Joong-sun had written his beloved girlfriend an apology letter because he flirted with another woman.

9. Mary Jane had told Susan lies many times before.

10. The Philippines had been battered by endless storms just in the last year.

Read the Examples below Very Carefully and Learn the Rules

1. It **had** flown over the cuckoo's nest before the bird jumped off the tree.
   Explanation: Had must be paired with **flown,** the participle verb, for the sentence to be right.

2. It **had** been difficult to speak to them lately.
   Explanation: It can stand in as a general subject.

3. It **had** become way too difficult to get along with you lately because of your bad behavior.
   Explanation: Had must be paired with the verb participle verb **become**.

4. They **had met** their new teachers from last year's English class.
   Explanation: **Had** must be paired with the verb participle **met** for your sentence to be correct.

5. They **had** known that learning English would be difficult.
   Explanation: Had is paired with participle [**known**]. This is correct.

6. They **had** made it to their destination.
   Question: Are the verbs paired correctly? Check your participle verb list.

7. They **had** done the most serious crime in school for not telling the principal the true story.
   Question: Are **had** and **done** paired correctly?

8. They **had** sold their house last month and moved on to another country.
   Explanation: Check your participle list to see if **had** can be paired with **sold**.

Hint: You must pair **had** to a **participle verb** in your sentence for it to be grammatically correct. The past tense verb **had** must marry the *participle verb*—there are no options. See the list of verb participle on pages 66–70 and use them in your sentences.

Now, I think it's your turn to write your own examples on a separate sheet of paper or in your notebook. The practice examples in the exercise below will help you understand what you have learned in this lesson.

Lesson Ten Exercise Two

Directions: You must pair the base verb [have] to the past-participle verb. Refer to your past participle verbs list and answer the questions on the blank lines. Remember that you are studying things or events that are already finished and done and describing them with the verb |had|.

1. I had _____ [drive] the new truck before it got slammed on the ditch.

2. Hoon-sun had _____ [fall] in love with his close friend, but he found out she was seeing someone else.

3. Everybody had _____[go] to the meeting when the ordered pizza was delivered.

4. We had _____ [clean] the kitchen when the maids arrived.

5. They had _____ [catch] a giant tuna fish in the Pacific Ocean before the tsunami storm happened.

6. You had _____ [sit] on that throne before because you felt entitled.

7. We had _____ [fight] all night long because my husband confessed he committed another adultery.

Now check your answers in the appendix to see if they are correct.

More on past and participle tenses: |has|, |is|, |was|, |were|.

Rules: You need to follow the past tense grammar rules—the same tense rule you read in Lesson Two. You need to pair |has|, |was|, |were|, and |is| with past participle verbs and add |-d| and |-ed| to a verb to create the past tense to describe our finished event.

Sentence examples:

1. She **has traveled** to California in the past and met Mickey Mouse at Disney World Florida. The subject **she** in this sentence is followed by the past tense verb travel**ed** by adding -**ed** to the base verb **travel**.

2. He **has taken** my heart before, but I won't let him fool me again. The **has** is followed by participle verb = **taken** [**take**]. See the participle list on pages 66–70.

3. That **was used** by my English teacher last semester. The verb **was** must be followed by **used** = past participle verb.

4. He **has found** Jesus' long-lost Holy Grail hidden in the cavern in Israel. The verb **has** is paired with **found** [participle verb]. You have to pair the two so that your sentence is correct.

Complete sentence: King Arthur **has created** a golden city in his kingdom. The present tense **has** is paired with the participle verb **created**.

Queen Guinevere's diamond tiara **is kept** in the vault. The verb **[is]** is followed by participle **kept**.

Ferdinand Magellan **was lost** at sea in search of a new land for the queen of Spain. The past tense **was** must be followed by participle **lost** to be correct because you are talking or writing about event in the past time.

They **were gone** [go] already by the time I arrived to the baby shower. The sentence has a plural subject and must have a plural verb in the past tense. **They** = subject and **were** = plural verb in the past tense.

Now, let's learn about apostrophes in your sentences.

Rule for apostrophe in your sentences [']:

An apostrophe is a sign that a person is the owner of the object or things being talked about in the sentence.

Example: My teacher's desk is full of books, rulers, erasers, paper punchers, pencils, pens, chalk, and family photos.

Explanation: The desk belongs to the teacher. The teacher is the owner of the desk and the apostrophe is a sign that the desk belongs to her.

Sentence: The pig's trough is full of leftover foods reserved for the winter.

Explanation: The word **pig's** has the apostrophe ['] after the letter [g] because the pig owns the trough—it's a box to hold food for animals.

Another meaning for **apostrophe:** Apostrophe is also a sign of two words becoming one single word called a **contraction**.

What is Contraction?

A contraction is the combining of two words into one |'|.

Example: I **will not** attend the graduation ceremony on Saturday. The verb and the word *not* can be joined together so that the **will not** becomes **won't**. Do you see the apostrophe between the letter |n| and |t|?

Put **won't** in your sentence: I **won't** attend the graduation ceremony on Saturday.

He **does not** run fast enough to compete in the Olympic Games in Brazil.

The **does not** can be shortened to **doesn't.** Do you see the apostrophe?

Example: He **doesn't** run fast enough to compete in the Olympic Games in Brazil.

Here is your assignment for tomorrow = **Here's** your assignment for tomorrow. The two words |here is| is shortened to |here's|.

It is a difficult class, but the teacher teaches well = **It's** a difficult class, but the teacher teaches well.

I am tired from working seven days a week = **I'm** tired from working seven days a week. **[I]** is the subject in this sentence and |am| is the verb.

Now let's move on to the next rule.

Mental Note: Do not count the word with the apostrophe in a sentence as a correct subject—this is wrong! Change the contraction to the two words to get the correct subject. Be careful as you choose the correct **subject-verb agreement.**

Example: I'm Mr. Apostrophe ['] and I can't be the subject in your sentence. Who is doing the talking in this sentence example? The subject is [I] and |am| is the verb. The sentence says that Mr. Apostrophe is not acceptable to use as your subject in your sentence. Now, let's write the correct sentence together.

An infinitive [to + verb] cannot be the verb in a sentence.

Mental Note: Do not count the possessive word with an apostrophe as the correct subject of a sentence. The word after the apostrophe in a possessive noun is the correct subject in the sentence.

Now, let's write the correct sentence with Mr. Apostrophe.

1. The school's design looks just like the ancient Roman architecture I saw in Europe. The *subject* in this complete sentence is **design**, not the school, and the verb is **looks**. It would not make sense to say or write it the sentence as: The school is design looks just like the ancient Roman architecture.

2. Another apostrophe example: The cat's toys are all over the dining room. It would not make sense to say: the cat is toys are all over the dining room. The sentence is wrong because the *subject-verb* rule agreement doesn't agree. A cat cannot be a toy [it's an animal] and the object [toys] for the cat must be plural |are| not [is]. This is an example of Mr. Apostrophe—a word in the possessive case in the sentence *cannot* be a subject, but the word after the apostrophe is the correct subject. Your subject in this sentence is: [toys] and the verb is [are].

3. The Wang's car = This is wrong. It cannot be read as: The Wang is car. You need to write or say it in complete sentence: The Wang's car is blue.

Do not confuse Mr. Apostrophe with contractions. In contractions, you are shortening or combining two words into one. For example, she's very tall = she is very tall.

Mental Note

- Remember that an infinitive [to + verb] cannot be a verb in a sentence.

Example:

I went to visit my aunt yesterday who lives on the farm = to visit [cannot be a verb]. The subject = I. The verb = went.

Another *No-No*. In English grammar, a *preposition* cannot be a subject. Here are some examples of prepositions: about, above, after, along, among, around, as, at, below, before, beneath, between, behind, beside, by, into, for, to, with. See more prepositions in the list on page 65.

- Do not confuse *prepositions* with *pronouns*. You can use a *pronoun* as the subject in your sentence. Some examples of pronouns are: anyone, anything, each, either, everybody, everyone, everything, neither, nobody, no one, somebody, someone, something, I, you, he, she, it, we. Each one can be a subject in your sentence.

Mental Notes

- You must remember to use the process of elimination.
- The process of elimination will help you locate the correct subject.
- After locating the correct subject, you will know the correct verb to use.

Predicate

What is a *predicate* in a sentence? The predicate tells us something about the subject. It tells us what action the subject is doing in the sentence; it describes the subject.

Lesson Review

Let's review our lessons.

Present Tense:

Example: The English teacher recommend her for the job [wrong].

Ask yourself: What is the subject in this sentence? The subject = English teacher. Next, ask yourself what is the verb? The verb in the sentence is recommend. Now that you know the subject and the verb, you need to decide where to add the **-s** because it is required in the present tense grammar rule. The **-s** should be added to the verb recommend: recommend becomes recommend**s** with an **-s** ending because the subject [English teacher] is singular [one person]. This sentence is in the third person present tense rule.

Grammatically correct: The English teacher recommend**s** her for the job.

Progressive verb

Another grammar rule: Progressive verb

Progressive Rule: You can add **-ing** to a **base verb** for present tense, past tense, and future tense when speaking [communication] or in formal essay writing for your sentences to be grammatically correct.

Read the examples: Adding **-ing** to verbs only.

I am **eat** now [base verb] becomes = I am eat**ing** now.

He is **run** [base verb] for a good cause = He is runn**ing** for a good cause.

She is **buy** [base verb] a new car = She is buy**ing** a new car.

It will be **rain** [base verb] tomorrow = it will be rain**ing** tomorrow.

It was **rain** [base verb] yesterday = it was rain**ing** yesterday.

Comparing sentences in different tenses:

I will be talk**ing** to her today after class = future tense

I am talk**ing** to her today after class = present tense

He was talk**ing** to her after our English class ended = past tense

They were talk**ing** to her after our English class ended = past tense plural

We were talk**ing** to her after our English class ended = past tense plural

He and she **were** talking to them after the teacher's meeting = plural subject **[he and she]** and plural past tense verb **[were]**. Both are in correct order agreement.

Rule for apostrophe in your sentence [']

An apostrophe is a sign that a person or persons are the owner or owners of the object or things being talked about in the sentence.

1. That desk is the teacher's table.

2. That is Yumi's book.

3. That is Chai's pen.

4. The bicycle is Alejandro's.

5. They found Jesus' holy grail in the cave.

6. Magellan's boat sank at sea.

7. That is Alejandro's backpack.

8. That is Edgar Degas's painting of France.

Talking Comments

Making a statement or saying a comment about something.

1. I was running in the rain yesterday.

2. I saw my teacher's car parked at the theater last night.

3. You were talking to Jessica when I called.

4. He is out jogging right now.

5. She is cleaning the kitchen.

6. It was raining hard at the mall yesterday.

7. "It will be raining again tomorrow," said the weather forecaster.

8. We are going to see a movie at the cinema.

9. They are leaving for Asia today.

10. She is a nice teacher.

11. California has a warm climate.

12. They live in the city.

13. The San Diego Zoo is a fun place to visit.

14. Disney Land is smaller than Disney World.

15. I don't like my school or my teachers.

Time to Practice

Now let's see how much you have learned from studying all the grammar rules.

Mental Note: Remember, in the United States, present tense, past tense, and future tense are called present perfect tense, past perfect tense, future perfect tense. The progressive tense is also called the continues tense. I purposely took out the word *perfect* from all four tenses to shorten the grammar rules identification so that you can remember each one easily. The word *perfect* in all three tenses simply means past tense.

Review Your Knowledge

Let's review what you have just studied. Complete the exercises on the following pages. Read the directions so that you know what tense to use and the correct verb. Take your time and concentrate on what you are doing. When you are finished, read each sentence to yourself aloud or with a friend. What you wrote down and read aloud will make long-term memory of the material easier. Check your answers on page 63.

Review Exercise One

Fill in the blanks with present tense verbs. Use the list on pages 66–70.

1. I should _____ my mother to remind her of her doctor's appointment.

2. I _____ to show you my new textbook.

3. Lorence _____ to Philip about his new red car.

4. Myong _____ a brand-new grandbaby.

5. Carlos _____ to talk on the phone for a long time.

6. Sarah _____ how to speak Spanish well.

7. Jose _____ a family visitor from Brazil.

8. Kyong _____ help with her English assignment.

9. Vicente _____ traveling abroad with his family.

10. Soledad _____ a Filipino woman from the Philippines.

11. Takero _____ to go fishing with his grandfather.

12. Patrick can _____ my lunch.

Review Exercise Two

Past Tense Rule: Add **-d** or **-ed** to base verbs to form the past tense. Fill in the blanks.

1. I hear _____ you have an A in your English class.

2. He walk _____ to school.

3. They move _____ to Japan.

4. She look _____ at me last night.

5. We attend _____ the school dance last year.

6. It move _____ with the rhythm.

7. The hotel reduce _____ the price of the room.

8. We enjoy _____ the show at the theater.

9. He echo _____ what the teacher said.

10. She repeat _____ the assignment instructions.

11. Hwan propose _____ marriage to the love of his life.

12. Lukas roast _____ a turkey for his friends.

Exercises: Short Stories

Directions: Read the short stories and fill in the blanks with the correct verb. There are seven short stories below for you to practice your grammar knowledge. Check your answers in the appendix.

Story One: Teena

Teena _____ just a teenager when I met her at the graduation ceremony. Teena _____ very friendly to me and my parents when her father _____ time to introduce her to us. After the ceremony, I _____ to look for her to congratulate her and to say goodbye. But I didn't see her anymore. By the time I _____ to where they _____ sitting down, they _____ already left.

54 • Lesson Review

One day, on a rainy afternoon, I _____ at the mall with a friend looking for an inexpensive tuxedo to wear for a wedding. To my _____ Teena _____ me and excitedly with a friendly smile reached out her hand to me for a handshake. I _____ her what she was doing at the mall on a rainy afternoon and she _____ she _____ there with friends to see a movie. The movie theater _____ not far from the mall. I _____ her to my friend Ben and Teena _____ a very nice girl who _____ not in such a hurry to leave. She _____ why I _____ looking for a tuxedo attire. I _____ her the tuxedo _____ for Ben's wedding. Teena _____ I was the groom. I _____ her what movie she and her friends are going to _____. She _____ they wanted to see *Pinocchio*. While Ben _____ busy looking around, Teena _____ if I was _____ or taking college classes. I _____ her I _____ a part-time job doing errands for an executive of a rich company. When she left, she _____ me to have a wonderful time at Ben's wedding.

Story Two: My Grandparents' Farm

Last summer I _____ to visit my grandparents at the farm with my younger sister. My grandparents _____ caring people and my favorite family members to visit. My grandfather _____ chickens in their backyard. I _____ playing with the chickens because they are friendly and they don't _____ away when I touch their feathers. I _____ 12 eggs in the chickens' house and I _____ them to my younger sister Juanita. She _____ the 12 eggs to grandmother to _____ for breakfast. Grandfather _____ happy to _____ us _____ the eggs for breakfast.

Story Three: My Happy Day

Today _____ my birthday. I am 8 years old. My parents _____ some of my school friends and the children in my neighborhood to help me _____ my special day. I am very happy to _____ Emily come to my party. She _____ a good friend of mine. Emily _____ me a birthday present and _____ me for _____ her at my party. I _____ her she's most _____.

Story Four: Going to Church

Every Sunday my older brother and I _____ to church with our parents. My mother _____ us up early to get there on time. Even though I don't _____ to wake up early, I _____ excited to go because my parents _____ us to a good restaurant for lunch after the church service. My favorite drink to order _____ a glass of lemonade with a hot plate of fried chicken. Besides the fried chicken, the hot plate _____ rice, okra, carrots, and rice pudding for dessert. My mother _____ happy when she _____ me _____ my meal.

Story Five: Trip to Korea

My Aunt Lucille lives and _____ in Korea as a teacher. One summer my father _____ me with a plane ticket to visit Aunt Lucille for a few weeks. I _____ never been to Korea or to any country overseas. Korea was my first country to visit abroad and I _____ very excited. My mother _____ me out shopping at the mall for summer cool clothes to wear for the trip. She _____ me a pair of light jeans, T-shirt, shorts, sunglasses, flip-flops, and a very huge luggage bag. The luggage my mother bought _____ bigger than my size. She _____ I _____ a bigger size luggage to fit everything in for the overseas trip. I _____ my mother I _____ fit in perfectly inside the luggage. My mother _____ ship the luggage with me inside and father could get a refund and _____ the money. My mother _____ my joke _____ not that funny at all, but she _____ me a nice smile.

Story Six: My New Bicycle

When I _____ seven years old my parents _____ me a bicycle. I loved my surprise Christmas present. I _____ to my friend Paolo's house to _____ him my new bicycle. But when I got to his house, they _____ already left for grocery shopping. I went to Cheng's house instead and I _____ him playing ping-pong with Nena. I _____ them my bicycle and _____ them my parents _____ it to me for Christmas. My friends _____ just as happy as I was and we took _____ riding my new bike.

Story Seven: English Communication Practice

Direction: Invite a friend or a family member to practice this short conversation, between Anna and Caspian, with you.

Anna: How are you Caspian?

Caspian: I'm fine. Thank you. How about you, Anna?

Anna: I'm okay, but I can't go to the dance with you tomorrow.

Caspian: Why not?

Anna: I don't feel very well.

Caspian: I'm sorry to hear that. I'll ask Aurora if she's available.

Anna: Yeah, I guess you will have to do that now. I'm sorry.

Caspian: Well, I'm sorry too. I hope you feel better soon.

Anna: I hope I will too. Have fun with Aurora at the dance.

Caspian: I'm sure I will. Bye now!

Anna: Goodbye!

56 • Lesson Review

Now let's practice short writing: Put your grammar knowledge to the test. Just as you need to pair the helping verbs with the participle verbs to be grammatically correct, you must do the same thing with the rules that you just studied and apply your knowledge to short writing passages. This process is called application: You will apply what you have learned from every lesson to writing—to see if you understand the rules correctly.

Writing Practice for Beginners

Let's learn how to write together. But before you start, read the story below very slowly. Use the words below to write your own short sentences. For a beginner English learner, you have to put your knowledge in writing from every lesson in this book. Through writing, you will know how much English you understood from your study. The exercise will also help you assess what you still need to learn. Take all the time you need and do not get impatient with yourself if you find writing sentences too hard. Concentrate on the *tense* because the tense will tell you the correct verb to use in your sentence.

Mental Note: Remember, the subject of a sentence can be the name of a person or persons, things, objects, |they|, |he|, |she|, |it|, |those|, |that|, |who|, |what|, and so on. These are just some of the many words that can be subject in a sentence. The verb in your sentence must agree with the subject. Show your finished writing to someone you know can help you correct your grammar. There is *no answer key* in this book for your writing practice—prewrite as many sentences as you like.

To start, I created a sample writing for you. Pay close attention to connecting words like |and|, |in|, |on|, |of|, |because|, |or|, |to|, |but|. I will use these connecting words in my short writing below. Use the vocabulary word list on pages 66–70 to help you put together a simple sentence. The connecting words cannot be used as a subject—you have to put a bracket around the connecting words to help you locate the correct subject. This process of elimination will help you find the correct subject more easily and then use the right verb.

Directions: Read the short story below and learn.

Short essay: An Exchange Student in Mexico (Writing Sample)

Sung-min is an exchange student from Korea who stayed with Roberto and his family in Mexico. Sung-min **and** Roberto met each other in Mexico in 2014 when Sung-min and her family were vacationing in Mexico. Sung-min arrived in Mexico in the summertime. Sung-min lived with Roberto's family as an exchange student for one year and attended school. Roberto introduced soccer to Sung-min on week-ends. The soccer game is called al futbol in Spanish. The two of them practiced playing al futbol **in** the meadow for one year. One Saturday Roberto took Sung-min to the community market after the soccer practice. The market is called el Mercado in Mexico **or** sijung in Korean.

A month before Sung-min left for her home country, Roberto wanted to take Sung-min to a game of the very popular Mexican sport of al futbol. **Of** all the Mexican sports Roberto showed Sung-min during her visit, Roberto thought Sung-min enjoyed soccer the least **but** he was wrong. He believed Sung-min would rather go to Hacienda Restaurant to enjoy Mexican food where Roberto and his parents once took Sung-min for dinner.

Directions: Now it's your turn to add more words to the second paragraph. Use the connecting words and all the words on pages 65–75 for help. If you feel that my paragraph is too long, rewrite it. Have someone in your family check your writing when you are finished. If you know someone who is good in English, show your paper to him or her for grammar correction and feedback.

Use the following table as your grammar guide.

Subject	Verb	Predicate
The giraffe	has	a long neck.
Those birds	are singing	in the trees.
I	went	to school.
Chai	is	tall.
They	raised	cows last year.
There	is	one squirrel in the orchard.
There	are	two apples on the tree.
My mother	was	cleaning the kitchen.
My friends	were	at my house last night.
He	had	two bicycles last year.
We	have	a boat.
The teacher	is	talking.
The baby	cries	all night long.
She	likes	beautiful flowers.

The table shows subject-verb agreement in all the sentences. The rest of the sentence |predicate| is explaining what each subject is doing. You will write about the subject only and will report what the subject is about. Don't forget to put a period at the end of your sentence.

Lesson Review

Writing can be very complicated. This book is written for beginner English learners and contains many examples for you to learn from—use it as your guide to correct writing. Now you start writing simple and short sentences on a separate sheet of paper or in your notebook. Use a dictionary or a language translator to help you if necessary. Do not worry about correct spelling or commas right now. Apply what you have learned so far to your writing to assess how much you already know and don't know yet. As you get comfortable with the rules of grammar, your writing and talking [communication] will soon sound correct—guaranteed!

APPENDIX

ANSWER KEYS

Lesson One Practice

1. Subject = birds. Verb = are singing.
2. Subject = I. Verb = hope.

Lesson One Exercise One

1. Subject = groom. Verb = is.
2. Subject = Lucinda. Verb = looks.
3. Subject = bridesmaids. Verb = are.
4. Subject = ring bearer. Verb = is.
5. Subject = flower girl. Verb = is.

Lesson Two Practice

1. Subject: |I|. Verb: |choose|. Tense: present.
2. Subject: |I|. Verb: |sill choose|. Tense: future
3. Subject: |I|. Verb: |chose|. Tense: past
4. Subject: |I|. Verb: |had chosen|. Tense: past

Lesson Two Exercise

1. Subject: |I|. Verb: |see|. Tense: present
2. Subject: |I|. Verb: |saw|. Tense: past
3. Subject: |I|. Verb: |had seen|. Tense: past
4. Subject: |She|. Verb: |will grow|. Tense: present
5. Subject: |He|. Verb: |grew|. Tense: past
6. Subject: |They|. Verb: |have grown| Tense: past
7. Subject: |We|. Verb: |like|. Tense: present
8. Subject: |It|. Verb: |grows|. Tense: present

9. Subject: |My sister|. Verb: |is going|. Tense: future
10. Subject: |We|. Verb: |like|. Tense: present

Lesson Three Exercise One

1. Subject |I|. Verb: |am going|. Tense: present.
2. Subject |I|. Verb: |am going|. Tense: future.
3. Subject |I|. Verb: |was going|. Tense: past.
4. Subject |He|. Verb: |was running|. Tense: past.
5. Subject |He|. Verb: |is talking|. Tense: present.
6. Subject |She|. Verb: |is leaving|. Tense: present.
7. She was leaving the party when the visitors arrived.
8. Subject |They|. Verb: |are working|. Tense: present.
9. Subject |They|. Verb: |were working|. Tense: past.
10. Subject |It|. Verb: |is jumping|. Tense: present.

Lesson Four Exercise

1. were
2. was
3. were
4. was
5. were
6. was
7. was

Lesson Five Exercise

1. rains
2. leaves
3. sees
4. speaks
5. sings
6. care
7. speak
8. walk
9. asks
10. appears

Lesson Six Exercise

1. likes
2. bathes
3. talks
4. works
5. cuts
6. cleans
7. mops
8. teaches
9. seems
10. appears
11. flies
12. smiles

Lesson Seven Exercise One

1. are
2. is
3. is
4. are
5. are
6. is
7. are
8. is
9. is
10. are

Lesson Seven Exercise Two

1. is
2. is
3. is
4. is
5. are
6. are
7. are

Lesson Nine Exercise

1. have
2. have
3. have
4. have
5. have
6. have
7. have
8. have
9. have
10. have
11. have
12. have

Lesson Ten Exercise One

1. Subject is [I]; the verb is [had].
2. [I] is paired with [had]. They must be together in the sentence to be correct.
3. [had] is paired with the verb participle [sung].
4. [had] is paired with the past participle verb [broken]. This is a correct sentence.
5. [had] is paired with the verb participle [hidden].
6. [had] must be paired with the verb participle [sworn] for the sentence to be grammatically correct.
7. The verb [had] is paired correctly with the verb participle [seen]. The sentence is grammatically correct.
8. [had] is paired with the verb participle [written].
9. [had] is paired with [told]; the sentence is correct.
10. [had] is paired with [been battered].

Lesson Ten Exercise Two

1. driven
2. fallen
3. gone
4. cleaned

5. caught
6. caught
7. sat
8. fought

Review Exercise One

1. call
2. want
3. talked
4. has
5. likes
6. knows
7. has
8. wants
9. is
10. is
11. wants
12. have

Review Exercise Two

1. heard
2. walked
3. moved
4. looked
5. attended
6. listened
7. reduced
8. enjoyed
9. echoed
10. repeated
11. proposed
12. baked

Exercises: Short Stories

Story One: Teena: was; was; took; went; got/arrived; were; had; was; surprise; saw; asked; said; was; was; introduced; was; was; asked; why; was; told; was; thought; asked; see; said; was; asked; working; told; had; told

Story Two: My Grandparents' Farm: went; are; raises; like; run; found; showed; gave; cook; was; see; enjoying

Story Three: My Happy Day: is; invited; celebrate; see; is; brought/gave; thanked; having; told; welcome

Story Four: Going to Church: go; wakes; like; am take; is; has; is; sees; finish

Story Five: Trip to Korea: works; surprised; have; was; took; bought; was; said; needed; told; would; could; save; thought; was; gave

Story Six: My New Bicycle: was; bought; went; show; had; found; showed; told; gave; were; turns

Word Lists

Connecting Words List

| and, but, or, of, in, on, | with, for, by, to, for, | besides, because, at |

Vocabulary Word List: Prepositions

aboard	about	above	across	after
against	along	amid	among	around
at	before	behind	below	beneath
beside	between	beyond	by	down
during	except	for	from	in
into	like	near	of	off
on	onto	out	over	past
since	through	throughout	to	toward
under	underneath	until	unto	up
upon	with	within	without	

List of Connecting Words: The Conjunctions

and	as	after	although
before	because	but	except
like	now	nor	once
or	if	than	that
though	so	Since	when
while	where	whether	unless
until			

List of Base Verbs

awake	blow	come	fall	get
be	break	dig	feel	give
beat	bring	do	fight	go
become	build	draw	find	grow
begin	burn	dream	fly	hang
bend	buy	drive	forget	have
bet	catch	drink	forgive	hear
bite	choose	eat	freeze	hide
hold	hurt	keep	know	lay
lead	learn	leave	lend	let
lie	lose	make	mean	meet
pay	put	read	ride	ring
rise	run	say	see	sell
send	show	shut	sing	sink
sit	sleep	speak	spend	stand
stink	swim	take	teach	tear
tell	think	throw	understand	wake
wear	win	write	hit	dig
cut	bid	bet	be	broadcast

Irregular Verb: Conjugated

Present Tense	**Past Tense**	**Past Participle Tense**
agree	agreed	agreed
appear	appeared	Appeared
ask	asked	asked
be	were	been
become	became	become
begin	began	begun

Present Tense	Past Tense	Past Participle Tense
believe	believed	believed
break	broke	broken
bring	brought	brought
build	built	build
buy	bought	bought
call	called	called
carry	carried	carried
catch	caught	caught
change	changed	changed
choose	chose	chosen
come	came	come
consider	considered	considered
continue	continued	continued
cover	covered	covered
create	created	created
cut	cut	cut
decide	decided	decided
develop	developed	developed
die	died	died
do	did	done
draw	drew	drawn
eat	ate	Eaten
explain	explained	explained
fall	fell	fallen
feel	felt	felt
find	found	found
follow	followed	followed
get	got	gotten

(*Continued*)

Present Tense	Past Tense	Past Participle Tense
give	gave	given
go	went	gone
grow	grew	grown
happen	happened	happened
have	had	had
hear	heard	heard
help	helped	helped
hit	hit	hit
hope	hoped	hoped
include	included	included
keep	kept	kept
kill	killed	killed
know	knew	know
lead	led	led
lean	learned	learned
leave	left	left
let	let	let
live	lived	lived
lose	lost	lost
make	made	made
mean	meant	meant
meet	met	met
move	moved	moved
need	needed	needed
offer	offered	offered
open	opened	opened
pass	passed	passed
pay	paid	paid

Present Tense	Past Tense	Past Participle Tense
play	played	played
produce	produced	produced
put	put	put
raise	raised	raised
reach	reached	reached
read	read	read
receive	received	received
remember	remembered	remembered
return	returned	returned
run	ran	run
say	said	said
see	saw	seen
seem	seemed	seemed
sell	sold	sold
send	sent	sent
serve	served	served
set	set	set
show	showed	shown
sit	sat	sat
speak	spoke	spoken
spend	spent	spent
stand	stood	stood
stay	stayed	stayed
stop	stopped	stopped
support	supported	supported
take	took	taken
teach	taught	taught
tell	told	told

(*Continued*)

Present Tense	Past Tense	Past Participle Tense
think	thought	Thought
try	tried	tried
understand	understood	understood
use	used	used
walk	walked	walked
want	wanted	wanted
watch	watched	watched
win	won	won
work	worked	worked
write	wrote	written

List of Regular Verbs

accept	amuse	applaud	attach
add	analyze	appreciate	attack
admire	announce	approve	attempt
admit	annoy	argue	attend
advise	answer	arrange	attract
afford	apologize	arrest	avoid
agree	appear	arrive	
alert		ask	
allow			
back	beg	boil	branch
bake	behave	bolt	breathe
balance	belong	bomb	bruise
ban	bleach	book	brush
bang	bless	bore	bubble
bare	blind	borrow	bump
bat	blink	bounce	burn
bathe	blot	bow	bury
battle	blush	box	buzz
beam	boast	brake	

calculate	choke	compare	cough
call	chop	compete	count
camp	claim	complain	cover
care	clap	complete	crack
carry	clean	concentrate	crash
carve	clear	concern	crawl
cause	clip	confess	cross
challenge	close	confuse	crush
change	coach	connect	cry
charge	coil	consider	cure
chase	collect	consist	curl
cheat	colour	contain	curve
check	comb	continue	cycle
cheer	command	copy	
chew	communicate	correct	
dam	deliver	disapprove	dress
damage	depend	disarm	drip
dance	describe	discover	drop
dare	desert	dislike	drown
decay	deserve	divide	drum
deceive	destroy	double	dry
decide	detect	doubt	dust
decorate	develop	drag	
delay	disagree	drain	
delight	disappear	dream	
earn	end	excite	explain
educate	enjoy	excuse	explode
embarrass	enter	exercise	extend
employ	entertain	exist	
empty	escape	expand	
encourage	examine	expect	

(*Continued*)

face	fetch	flash	force
fade	file	float	form
fail	fill	flood	found
fancy	film	flow	frame
fasten	fire	flower	frighten
fax	fit	fold	fry
fear	fix	follow	
fence	flap	fool	
gather	grab	grin	guard
gaze	grate	grip	guess
glow	grease	groan	guide
glue	greet	guarantee	
hammer	harm	heat	hug
hand	hate	help	hum
handle	haunt	hook	hunt
hang	head	hop	hurry
happen	heal	hope	
harass	heap	hover	
identify	increase	intend	invite
ignore	influence	interest	irritate
imagine	inform	interfere	itch
impress	inject	interrupt	
improve	injure	introduce	
include	instruct	invent	
jail	jog	joke	juggle
jam	join	judge	jump
kick	kiss	knit	knot
kill	kneel	knock	
label	learn	lighten	load
land	level	like	lock
last	license	list	long
laugh	lick	listen	look
launch	lie	live	love

man manage march mark marry match mate	matter measure meddle melt memorize mend mess up	milk mine miss mix moan moor mourn	move muddle mug multiply murder
nail name	need nest	nod note	notice number
obey object observe	obtain occur offend	offer open order	overflow owe own
pack paddle paint park part pass paste pat pause peck pedal peel peep perform permit	phone pick pinch pine place plan plant play please plug point poke polish pop	possess post pour practice pray preach precede prefer prepare present preserve press pretend	prevent prick print produce program promise protect provide pull pump punch puncture punish push
question	queue		

(*Continued*)

race	refuse	remove	rhyme
radiate	regret	repair	rinse
rain	reign	repeat	risk
raise	reject	replace	rob
reach	rejoice	reply	rock
realise	relax	report	roll
receive	release	reproduce	rot
recognise	rely	request	rub
record	remain	rescue	ruin
reduce	remember	retire	rule
reflect	remind	return	rush
sack	shiver	soothe	stop
sail	shock	sound	store
satisfy	shop	spare	strap
save	shrug	spark	strengthen
saw	sigh	sparkle	stretch
scare	sign	spell	strip
scatter	signal	spill	stroke
scold	sin	spoil	stuff
scorch	sip	spot	subtract
scrape	ski	spray	succeed
scratch	skip	sprout	suck
scream	slap	squash	suffer
screw	slip	squeak	suggest
scribble	slow	squeal	suit
scrub	smash	squeeze	supply
seal	smell	stain	support
search	smile	stamp	suppose
separate	smoke	stare	surprise
serve	snatch	start	surround
settle	sneeze	stay	suspect
shade	sniff	steer	suspend
share	snore	step	switch
shave	snow	stir	
shelter	soak	stitch	

talk	thaw	trace	trot
tame	tick	trade	trouble
tap	tickle	train	trust
taste	tie	transport	try
tease	time	trap	tug
telephone	tip	travel	tumble
tempt	tire	treat	turn
terrify	touch	tremble	twist
test	tour	trick	type
thank	tow	trip	
undress	unite	unpack	use
unfasten	unlock	untidy	
vanish	visit		
wail	waste	whirl	work
wait	watch	whisper	worry
walk	water	whistle	wrap
wander	wave	wink	wreck
want	weigh	wipe	wrestle
warm	welcome	wish	wriggle
warn	whine	wobble	
wash	whip	wonder	
x-ray			
yawn	yell		
zip	zoom		

Let's Talk about Nouns

What is a noun? A *noun* is used in a sentence in more ways than one. Look at the table shown on page 57 and see if they look familiar to you. What comes to your mind just by looking at the table? Do the words remind you of subjects that can be used in a sentence? The answer is yes!

For example, read this sentence: The tiger ran after the zebra. In this sentence, tiger and zebra are nouns, and the |tiger| is also the subject in that sentence. Another sentence: He decided to go to the theater. The noun in this sentence is |He|. The noun |He| is also the subject in that sentence. For that reason, there is no benefit for you to have to remember whether a sentence must have a subject pronoun or an object pronoun.

The current and most common definition of a noun is this: A *noun* is a word that denotes a person, place, or thing.

In Lesson One you have learned that an object can be a subject just as a person or |it| a |thing| can be a subject in a complete sentence. They are all *nouns*. For this reason, there is no need for you to remember whether a complete sentence must have a subject pronoun or an object pronoun.

By English grammar definition, a complete sentence must have a *subject* and a *verb* and the two must *agree* in *tense* for the sentence to be correct. With that understanding, let us learn our grammar by following the English correct grammar definition.

Examples of a complete and correct simple sentences: |I sing|, |I walk|, |I dance|, |I bathe|, |I listen|, |I run|, |I cook|, and so much more. Where is the subject? The subject in all the examples is |I|, and the verb is what the subject |I| does in each sentence. Can you find the verb in each sentence?

Past Tense

Examples: |I sang|, |I walked|, |I danced|, I bathed|, |I listened|, |I ran|, |I cooked|.

Because this book is designed for beginner English learners, we will do away with sophisticated sentence construction. Later, as you become more comfortable with your English, you may want to use flowery words in your writing. For now, let's learn the basic building blocks of English grammar by writing and by talking.

Examine the table below.

Subject and Object Pronouns	
Subject Pronouns	*Object Pronouns*
I	me
we	us
you	you
she	her

Subject and Object Pronouns	
Subject Pronouns	*Object Pronouns*
he	him
it	it
they	them

Remember, *prepositions* cannot be the subjects of any sentence. With that understanding, we have to take out the *preposition words* in the sentence. Do the same for conjunctions in a sentence—conjunctions cannot be used as subjects. See the prepositions and conjunction lists at the end of this book.

Here is how you take out the prepositions and conjunctions, via a process of elimination:

Sentence 1: Hawaii became the fiftieth state of the United States in 1959. Take out: [of the United States] = Hawaii became the fiftieth state in 1959. The subject is [Hawaii] and the verb is [became]. The preposition |of| is taken out.

Sentence 2: One of many islands of the Caribbean is controlled by the French government. Take out [of many islands of the Caribbean] = One is controlled by the French government. The subject is [One]. The verb is |is|. The preposition |of| is taken out.

Follow these simple steps and your English sentences should be correct.

Mental Hint

Where is the subject?	What is the sentence about?
	Who is the sentence about?
	Who is talking in the sentence?
Where is the verb?	The verb is the action in the sentence.
	See more about verbs on pages 66–75.

Topics to Write About: List of Suggestions

How to play basketball

The four seasons in Southeast Asia

How to cook spaghetti

How to bargain in the open market

How to play a guitar

How to play a piano

My favorite book

Why is immoral behavior unacceptable?

About religion
Other cultures
How to bake a cake
Politics and government
How to raise children
How to feed a hummingbird
How to care for a bulldog
How to fix a broken computer
How to fix a broken car engine
How to play an instrument

How to Ask Questions in the Present Tense

Mental Note: When asking questions, use the present tense form.

Table A.1

Who . . .	What . . .	When . . .	Where . . .	How . . .
Are you . . .	Do you . . .	Could you . .	Would you . . .	
Why . . .	Have . . .	Has . . .		

This table is a list of words that you can use when asking general questions. Your questions must include a base verb in the present tense form.

Question: Who . . . ?

Who is your teacher?
Who is that boy sitting next to you?
Who can help me with my English assignment?
Who do you want to speak with?
Who is the teacher?
Who are you looking for?
Who should I talk to?

Question: What . . . ?

What room are you in?
What class are you in?
What can I do for you?

What is our assignment today?
What kind of book is that?
What do you want to do after class?
What is your favorite thing to do on weekends?
What books are we using in this class?
What is the title of your textbook?
What time does the class start?
What country are you from?
What language do you speak?
What do you suggest I do?

Question: When . . . ?
When do you leave for work?
When do you leave home for school?
When would you like us to go to the market together?
When can you call me today?
When are you going home to your country?
When are you going back home?
When can I see you?

Question: Where . . . ?
Where do you live?
Where is the library?
Where do I catch the bus?
Where do you study?
Where do you shop for groceries?
Where is your book?
Where is my book?
Where is the teacher?
Where did you park?
Where do you go out to eat?
Where are your parents?
Where is your husband?
Where is your wife?
Where is your girlfriend?

Question: How . . . ?

    How old are you?

    How much English do you already know?

    How do you go home from school?

    How far is your home from here?

    How much money do you have?

    How many children do you have?

    How much money do you want to spend at the mall?

    Who is your teacher this semester?

Question: Are you . . . ?

    Are you single?

    Are you married?

    Are you from Mexico?

    Are you from Asia?

    Are you from the Middle East?

    Are you from Europe?

    Are you from Africa?

    Are you from the Mongolia?

    Are you Spanish?

    Are you happy?

    Are you sad?

    Are you thirsty?

    Are you hungry?

    Are you bilingual?

    Are you smart?

    Are you married?

    Are you pregnant?

    Are you from around here?

Question: Do you . . .

    Do you want to practice your English with me?

    Do you have a car?

    Do you ride a bus home?

    Do you like to cook?

    Do you like to go shopping?

Do you have friends here?
Do you have a good neighbor?
Do you like to sing karaoke?
Do you like to write?
Do you drive?
Do you have children?
Do you want me to drive you home?
Do you like to eat American food?
Do you like going to the library?
Do you need a roommate?
Do you have money?

Question: Could you . . .

Could I bring you something from the library?
Could you please help me carry my books to class?
Could you please bring me a drink?
Could you please buy me a drink from the machine?
Could you please buy me the bus ticket?
Could you please buy my lunch at the cafeteria?

Question: Would you . . .

Would you please be quiet?
Would you please pick up that paper on the floor?
Would you mind lending me a paper?
Would you mind if I borrow a paper from you?
Would you be kind enough to lend me a dollar?
Would please give me a call home after class?
Would you like me to help you do your assignment?
Would you like to taste my food?
Would you like a drink?
Would you like us to share the apartment?
Would you like to see a movie with me?
Would you like to go with me to the park?
Would you mind if I ride home with you?
Would you please call me when you are ready?
Would you share a ride home with me?

Question: Why . . .

    Why do I have to give you money?

    Why can't you do the reading first?

    Why have you not taken the test yet?

    Why can't I come to your apartment?

    Why does she have to take you home?

Question: Have . . .

    Have you been to the zoo?

    Have you seen the Disney movie?

    Have they started the class yet?

    Have you had lunch yet?

    Have we gone mad?

    Have you done your assignment?

    Have you been to the mall?

Question: Has . . .

    Has your message been delivered?

    Has he been to your apartment?

    Has the plane left?

    Has the house sold?

    Has the cat found a mouse?

Would you like to . . .

    Would you like to go with me to the park?

    Would you mind if I ride home with you?

    Would you please call me when you are ready?

    Would you share a ride home with me?

How to Answer Questions

Question: Where do you live?

Answer: I live at 3232 Summit Way, Stafford, Virginia.

Q: Can I drive you home?

A: Yes, you can. I don't have a car.

Q: Do you need help with your assignment?

A:	Yes, I need help with my assignment.
Q:	Do you want to come with me to the mall?
A:	Yes, I like to go to the mall with you.
Q:	Do you speak English?
A:	No, I don't speak good English.
A:	Yes, I speak English very well.
Q:	Where do you go to school?
A:	I go to the University of Virginia.
Q:	Are you married?
A:	No, I'm not married.
Q:	Are you single?
A:	Yes, I am single.
Q:	Who is your teacher?
A:	My teacher is Mrs. Quezon.

Reminders

Now that you understand how to write a simple sentence, it's time for you to put your knowledge into serious writing. Prewrite as many sentences as you like, but be sure to follow the grammar rules as your guide. If you are using Microsoft Word, count 5 spaces from left side of your paper before you begin writing. In English, you write from left to right. A paragraph is usually about five to eight sentences. You need to indent again to start your *second* and *third* paragraph. The last paragraph is your third and final composition.

Select your own topic to write about. You may use any sample topics on pages 77–78 if you want. You need to capitalize the first letter of the word in your sentence and end it with a period—see page 84. Do not be concerned with perfecting your writing at this time. Put your focus on building to write correctly—in simple sentences. Carefully examine the sample writing on page 92.

Look out for these words in your sentences—they can be mistaken as subjects because they are positioned next to verbs in most cases. You will find the verb first followed by the subject: |there|, |here|, |where|, |what|, |which|, and |who|. Use Table A.2 to help you find the subject in your sentence.

Table A.2

there	here	where	what	which	who

Examples:

1. There *is* a good *movie* this week at the cinema. Look for the verb that comes first = is. The subject comes after the verb = movie.

2. Here are the flowers you wanted. Verb = are. Subject = flowers.

3. Where did you go to school? Verb = did. Subject = you.

4. What is your name? Subject = name. Verb = is.

5. Which is your apartment? Subject = apartment. Verb = is.

6. Who is your teacher this semester? Subject = teacher. Verb = is.

Table A.3 Singular Subject List: All Can Be Subjects

anyone	anything	each	either	everybody
everyone	everything	neither	nobody	no one
one	somebody	someone	something	

Table A.3 is a list of subjects that you can use in your sentence. They are called indefinite pronouns.

Examples:

1. *Anyone* of you *is* welcome to come to the school dance.

2. *Everyone is* invited to the picnic.

3. *One* pencil *is* all I need.

4. *Anything is* good for the goose.

5. *Everything is* already out there.

6. *Somebody is* having a birthday today.

7. *Neither* Susie nor John *has* improved their English.

8. *Someone is* getting married this Sunday.

9. *Either* Scott or Nelly *is going* to the carnival tonight.

10. *Nobody is learning* very well in that class.

11. *Something* wonderful *is going* to happen next week.

12. *No one is* above the law.

Mental Notes

- Can you circle the subject in the examples above?
- Can you underline the verb?
- Do you understand the predicate now?
- In your sentence, you are reporting or explaining what the subject is about—you are not writing about the verb.
- The verb tense must agree with your subject.

Application: Writing Practice

Lessons Review

A complete sentence: subject + verb + what the subject is about.

Ask yourself: What do I want to say or write about the subject?

Ask yourself: Am I talking or writing about present, past, or the future?

Mental Notes

- When you write a sentence, the subject in your sentence is the person or the object that the sentence is about. You will be talking about what the subject is doing in your sentence—not about the verb. The verb in the sentence tells what action the subject is doing in your sentence.
- The tense must be demonstrated with the right verb.
- You have to put a period at the end of your sentence.
- You have to capitalize the beginning of your sentence.
- You have to capitalize the names of people and animals.
- Do the process of elimination to find the correct subject.
- A word with an apostrophe cannot be the subject of any sentence.
- Conjunctions and prepositions cannot be the subject of a sentence.

Example: |They (subject)| |are going (verb)| to church on Sunday. The sentence is telling you that |they| are going to church on Sunday. In the same way, your sentence should tell or describe what the subject is doing. Just make sure your subject and verb agree in number and that the verb is written in the correct tense!

Example: Words like *today, yesterday, tomorrow, this week, next year, an hour ago, 15 minutes ago,* and so forth, will be part of your sentence. Be sure you have the right verb tense.

Correct sentence examples:

1. I like to play basketball = present tense.

    |I (subject)|. |Like (verb)|. Playing basketball is what the subject is doing. You will be reporting what the subject is doing in your sentence.

2. The boy is chasing the ball = present tense.

    |Boy (subject)|. |Is chasing (verb)|. |Ball (object)|.

3. My sister *will go* to the mall tomorrow = future tense.

    |My sister (subject)|. |Will go (verb)|. Mall = noun.

4. Pedro pl<u>ayed</u> basketball with Henry yesterday = past tense
   |Pedro (subject)|. |Played (past tense verb)|. Henry = noun.

Third person present tense rules (only): |-s|; |-ies|; |-es|.

Sentence Examples: Third Person Present Tense

Sentence examples: |-s|, |-ies|, |-es|.

1. She <u>write</u> books. It becomes = She write<u>s</u> books [correct].

2. The plane fly to Asia = It becomes: The plane f<u>lies</u> to Asia [correct].

3. It <u>simmer</u> when it is very hot = It becomes: It simmer<u>s</u> when it is very hot [correct].

4. He <u>cry</u> for a sad movie. It becomes: He cr<u>ies</u> for a sad movie [correct].

5. America <u>see</u> General George Washing as their courageous revolutionary American hero. It becomes: America see<u>s</u> General George Washington as their courageous revolutionary American hero.

6. It <u>change</u> the color of the sky. It becomes: It change<u>s</u> the color of the sky. The subject |It| might be the weather, the colors of a rainbow, rain, clouds, the season—might be the reason for the changed color of the sky.

Remember, |It| as the subject in the sentence is a "wild card"—you must figure |It| out so that your *verb tense* is correct. The |It (subject)| can be anything in the sentence—it can be an object.

Progressive Tense Verbs in a Sentence

1. I <u>like</u> play<u>ing</u> basketball = progressive verb |present tense (like playing)|.

2. My sister will <u>be</u> go<u>ing</u> to the mall tomorrow = progressive verb | future tense (will be going)|.

3. Pedro <u>was</u> play<u>ing</u> basketball with Henry yesterday = progressive verb |past tense (was playing)|.

Follow the verb tense examples below as your guide:

1. Future tense

2. Present tense

3. Past tense

4. Past participle: past perfect tense

5. Progressive tense: continuous tense

Examples: Guide

Future Tense

1. Scott *will go* to work tomorrow.

2. Jon *will be getting* married next month.

Present Tense

1. Odong *reads* a science book.

2. Kristina *is finishing* acting school this year.

Past Tense

1. We *went* to visit grandmother last summer.

2. He ask*ed* the teacher a question.

Past Participle Tense

1. I *had sung* at my barrio fiesta last year.

2. Donald *had shrunk* my new shirt after washing it in hot water.

Progressive (Continuous) Tense

Add -ing to base verb in all tenses!

1. The class *is going* to a field trip tomorrow to see Panda Bear at the zoo.

2. We *are having* dinner at my uncle's house tonight.

3. I *am going* to the library to borrow a book.

4. He *has been seeing* Sunny for over two years.

5. They *had been planning* to visit Manila since last year.

6. She *was leaving* the birthday party when I arrived.

7. It *can be frustrating* sometimes in my English class.

Lesson: Writing

Sample Writing: Read

Beginner Writing Composition

My favorite hobby is playing drums. I spend a lot of my free time playing drums. I started learning to play drums when I was 9 years old. I played in my school's band. When I was 12 years old, I had a private drum teacher and started to really enjoy playing.

My parents bought me a drum set and I started practicing every day after school. It was very loud, but my mother never complained. I improved a lot, and playing drums has been my favorite hobby ever since.

Now, I play drums in a band with my friend Dan, who plays guitar. We write songs, perform, and practice twice a week. It's still as fun as it was when I first started playing!

Let's think about writing and practice short writing now. Can you put in writing what you just learned from every lesson in this book? Because English grammar has so many rules that you must understand very well, it is my advice to you to put your knowledge in short writing so that your mind can retain them more eaisily and the rules can become second nature to you.

Tables A.4, A.5, and A.6 should help you identify the *subject* in your sentence and easily figure out the correct *verb tense* to use. For ESL students, these tables are extremely helpful for speaking and writing compound sentences.

Examples of compound sentences:

1. The duck was swimming in the pond, and the rat was with him.

2. Mrs. Flores plans to write more grammar books, and Mrs. Chang plans to continue teaching my English classes next semester.

3. I was going to attend your wedding, but a strong storm came and I could not make it.

4. Jose told me there was no homework to do because the teacher was out sick yesterday.

5. I found out that Sung could play the violin and that Miguel used to play the piano.

Table A.4 Subject Pronouns

	Subject Pronouns	
	Singular	**Plural**
First Person	I	we
Second Person	you	you
Third Person	he, she, it	they

Table A.5 Subject Verb Agreement and the Use of an Object in a Sentence

Subject	**Sentence**	**Object**	**Sentence**
I	I like Susie.	me	Eric likes me.
you	You like Susie.	you	Eric likes you.
he	He likes Susie.	him	Eric likes him.
she	She likes Susie.	her	Eric likes her.
it	It is awesome.	it	Eric loves it.
we	We like Susie.	us	Eric likes us.
they	They like Susie.	them	Eric likes them.

Table A.6 Guide for Using Prounouns

Pronoun as Subject	**Pronoun as Object**	**Possessive Pronoun**
I	me	mine
you	you	yours
he	him	his
she	her	hers
it	it	its
we	us	ours
you	you	yours
they	them	theirs

Sentence Building: Example

Directions: Choose any one of the sample sentences below and add your own words to them.

1. I like Rosa and I like Antonio.

2. I have an English book and a science book.

3. I have one brother and one sister.

4. She likes my backpack, but she doesn't like my pen.

5. She wants me to practice my English with her.

6. She is a nice girl, but she doesn't want to talk to me.

7. He is tall and handsome.

8. He likes to read, and he likes to sing.

9. He said his brother is an engineer and his sister is a nurse.

10. We wanted to ride the ferries wheel, but we had no money to buy the tickets.

11. We were not at the fiesta last night, but I wish we were there.

12. We play ping-pong on weekends, but my favorite game is soccer.

13. They have a swimming pool in their backyard, but it is very small.

14. They don't like to go swimming, but they like to bike on weekends at the park.

15. They said I can go swimming in their swimming pool and bring my friend Lisa.

16. Those soccer balls are ours; the team will have to return them to us.

17. The money I found on the floor is theirs; I should give it back to them.

18. The school campus and its students are pr.eparing for the annual festivals.

Mental Note

The grammar rules that you have learned in this book are for beginners, but the information you just learned, is very helpful for developing your English speaking, listening, reading, and writing proficiencies.

Dictionary: Confusing Words

1. accept = take

   He accepts advice from his parents.

   She has a problem accepting a bribe.

2. except = but

   Except for Toro, everyone accepted the grades.

3. advice = recommendation

   My advice to you is to participate in class.

   His advice to the students is to study harder for the test.

4. affect = change

   My low grade did not affect my desire to pass the class.

5. effect = result

   The effect of lying is misery.

6. already = in the past

   He already submitted his assignment.

7. all ready = completely prepared

   Yunso is all ready to take the exam.

8. among = surrounded by people or things

   He is among friends.

   The maple tree is the tallest among all trees in the forest.

9. between = for or from/to only two people or things

   Between the two of us your secret is safe.

   The problem is between the two of them.

   The distance between earth and sky is very far.

10. awhile = a short time

    You stay there awhile.

11. a while = used as object of preposition

    You stay there for a while.

12. beside = next to someone or something

    She sat beside him in the bus.

    I was sitting beside you on the train.

13. besides = an addition to

    Besides free cookies, drinks were also free.

    Besides Cecilia, Yolanda was enrolled in the same class.

    No one was in the house besides the maids.

14. brake = part of automobile, bicycle, truck, and so on

    The brake of my car is not working.

    My car brake broke down.

15. break = destroy

    Don't break that glass window.

16. course = 1 class

    I'm taking an English course.

17. coarse = rough

    The road full of potholes is coarse.

18. desert = hot and empty land

    The Gobi Desert is an arid land connecting China and Mongolia.

19. dessert = sugary food after a meal

    She had ice cream for dessert.

    The family had a cake for dessert after dinner.

20. every day = describe something normal [adverb]

    Bad weather doesn't happen every day.

21. every day = without missing a day

    I go to work every day.

    I wake up at 7:30 a.m. every day.

    The mail carrier stops by the house every day.

22. fewer = smaller count; smaller number of persons or things

    There were fewer people who attended the meeting.

    Fewer storms occurred last month than this month.

23. less = smaller in amount, for things that cannot be counted

    Less talk helps me concentrate better.

24. hear = to sense sounds through your ears

    I hear the school bell's ring.

    Did you hear the fire engine's siren?

25. here = a place or position

    Come here.

    Here is your report card.

26. hole = opening

    The golf course has 18 holes.

    There is a hole in that cave.

27. whole = the entire thing

    The whole earth is round.

    His whole family went to the zoo.

28. knew = past tense of *know*; understood clearly

    She knew he was married.

    The school knew I needed help.

29. new = never been used

    My bike is new.

    The school building is new.

30. know = present tense; fully aware

    Do you know how to ride a bicycle?

    I know my teacher is nice.

31. no = not acceptable

    No, you can't be absent.

    She said no, I can't take her to the dance.

32. loose = not tight

    My shirt is too loose on me.

    His belt is loose.

33. lose = fail to maintain possession

    Did he lose his assignment?

34. passed = past tense of pass; to pass by

    She passed the exam last week.

    Anita passed me in the hallway.

35. past = in the past time.

    They used to be my neighbor in the past.

    World Wars I and II happened in the past.

36. patience = calm behavior.

    I'm running out of patience with him.

    She taught her students with patience.

37. patients = people who need medical help

    Dr. Solis's patients at the hospital are very sick.

38. patient = remain calm

    Be patient with me please!

    I must be patient with a long line of people at the register.

39. peace = harmony; not war.

    My English class needs peace because it's too noisy.

    The world needs peace, not war.

40. piece = a slice or a piece of a whole

    I don't want the whole apple pie; I just want a piece of it.

41. plain = simple

    The lesson was plain to me.

42. plane = airplane

    I'm not travelling by train, but by plane.

    He will fly by plane to visit his grandparents.

43. principal = public school leader

    Eric's school principal is a man.

44. principle = what you believe in

    My principle is to behave right.

    His principle is immoral.

45. quiet = silence or very little sound

    Everybody must be quiet during the test.

    A noisy library must be quiet.

46. quite = very

    I'm quite sure she was absent.

47. right = correct

    Your answer on the test is right.

    Her report is right.

48. write = create language using a pen and paper or a computer

   Write a short essay.

   Write a paragraph.

49. tail = end part

   A fish has a tail.

   The elephant's tail is long.

   The dog's tail is wagging.

50. tale = a story

   The Cinderella tale is popular.

   The tale of Jesus is ancient.

51. than = compared to

   Your test grade is better than mine.

   She is taller than him.

52. then = at that time

   I was only a teenager then.

   You were just a child then.

53. though = despite

   Though I didn't want to read, I read anyway.

54. thought = past tense of think, thinking

   I thought her idea was helpful.

   The thought of taking a long exam is petrifying.

55. threw = past tense of *throw*; to hurl

   She threw the bad apple into the trashcan.

   He threw the ball over the fence at the game.

56. through = finished; going into and out the other end

   The bus went through the tunnel.

   Are you through with your test?

57. weather = state of the earth's atmosphere at any given time or place

   Today's weather is too hot.

   The weather is too cold.

   Yesterday's weather was too windy.

58. whether = if

   Tell me whether you know the answer or not.

   Do you know whether she will marry him or not?

59. were = past tense of *to be*

    Were you at the dance last night?

    We were at the cinema when you called.

60. where = location

    Where are you now?

    I went to school because that is the place where I need to be.

61. Who's = contraction of *who + is*

    Who's that pretty girl?

    Who's your teacher this semester?

62. whose = possessive case for *who*

    Whose ruler is that?

    Whose book is this?

How to Negate

Negation means saying no to what others are saying to you or describing something that you don't want to do. Say the word *no* first, followed by a comma (usually) if your sentence is in writing, and then say the rest of your sentence.

Examples:

Question: Would you like to go swimming today?

Answer: No, I don't want to go swimming today.

Question: Are you from China?

Answer: No, I'm from France.

Question: Do you like your English teacher?

Answer: No, I don't like my English teacher.

How to Say Yes in Answer to a Question

When you say yes to a question, it means that you approve of what a person is saying to you. You often need to say yes first before you say the rest of your sentence.

Examples:

Question: Do you like your reading class?

Answer: Yes, I like my reading class.

Question: Are you going to register for an English class next semester?

Answer: Yes, I'm going to register for an English class next semester.

Question: Did you buy your books?

Answer: Yes, I ordered my books last night online. (past tense verb)

Examples of Conjugations for Some Verbs

Practice: lose; loose; loss; losses; lost

Examples:

Lose: You could *lose* your house key if you don't keep it in a safe place.

Loose: My blue jeans are *loose*; I need a belt.

Loss: I sold my car at a *loss* to a friend.

Losses: Traders experienced some *losses* on the stock market today.

Lost: They *lost* their bikes yesterday.

Now, do some practice writing on your own using each word below. Be sure to use them correctly—in the correct tense. Write your sentences in one notebook so that you'll have them to as a reference when you study.

A

admit | admits | admitting | admitted |

advise | advises | advising | advised |

afford | affords | affording | afforded |

agree | agrees | agreeing | agreed |

allow | allows | allowing | allowed |

apologize | apologizes | apologizing | apologized |

appear | appears | appearing | appeared |

appreciate | appreciates | appreciating | appreciated |

arrange | arranges | arranging | arranged |

ask |asks | asking | asked |

attempt | attempts | attempting | attempted |

B

begin | begins | beginning | begun |
belong | belongs | belonging | belonged |
bike | bikes | biking | biked |
blow | blows | blowing | blown |
borrow | borrows | borrowing | borrowed |
break | breaks | breaking | broke | broken |
breathe | breathes | breathing | breathed |
bring | brings | bringing | brought |
broil | broils | broiling | broiled |
brush | brushes | brushing | brushed |

C

call | calls | calling | called |
carry | carries | carrying | carried |
cause | causes | causing | caused |
celebrate | celebrates | celebrating | celebrated |
challenge | challenges | challenging | challenged |
change | changes | changing | changed |
collect | collects | collecting | collected |
cost | costs | costing | costly | cost |
count | counts | counting | counted |
cry | cries | crying | cried |

D

delay | delays | delaying | delayed |
deliver | delivers | delivering | delivered |
depend | depends | depending | depended |

deposit | deposits | depositing | deposited |

describe | describes | describing| described |

design | designs | designing | designed |

desire | desires | desiring | desired |

destroy | destroys | destroying | destroyed |

determine | determines | determining | determined |

develop | develops | developing | developed |

E

eat | eats | eating | ate |

encourage | encourages | encouraging | encouraged |

establish | establishes | establishing | established |

estimate | estimates | estimating | estimated |

estimate | estimates | estimating | estimated |

evaluate | evaluates | evaluating | evaluated |

exchange | exchanges | exchanging | exchanged |

excuse | excuses | excusing | excused |

F

face | faces | facing | faced |

fail | fails | failing | failed |

fake | fakes | faking | faked |

fall | falls | falling | fallen |

favor | favors | favoring | favored |

fly| flies | flying | flew | flown |

forgive | forgives | forgiving | forgave |

freeze | freezes | froze | frozen |

fry | fries | frying | fried |

G

gather | gathers | gathering | gathered |
get | gets | getting | got | gotten |
give| gives | giving | given | gave |
go | goes | going | gone |
grab| grabs | grabbing | grabbed |
grill | grills | grilling | grilled |
groom | grooms | grooming | groomed |
grow | grows | growing | grown | grew |
guess | guesses | guessing | guessed |
guide | guides | guiding | guided |

H

happen | happens | happening | happened |
harass| harasses| harassing | harassed |
heal | heals | healing | healed |
heat | heats| heating | heated |
help | helps | helping | helped |
hold | holds | holding | held |
hope | hopes | hoping | hoped |
hug | hugs | hugging | hugged |
hurry | hurries | hurrying | hurried |
hurt | hurts | hurting | hurtful |

I

identify | identifies | identifying | identified |
ignore | ignores | ignoring | ignored |
improve | improves | improving | improved |
include | includes | including | included |

increase | increases | increasing | increased |

inform | informs | informing | informed |

insult | insults | insulting | insulted |

interest | interests | interesting | interested |

invent | invents | inventing | invented |

invite | invites | inviting | invited |

J

jams | jams | jamming | jammed |

jog | jogs | jogging | jogged |

join | joins | joining | joined |

joke | jokes | joking | joked |

judge | judges | judging | judged |

juggle | juggles | juggling | juggled |

jump| jumps | jumping | jumped|

K

keep | keeps | keeping | kept |

key | keys | keying | keyed |

kick | kicks | kicking | kicked |

kindle | kindles | kindling | kindled |

kiss | kisses | kissing | kissed |

knead | kneads | kneading | kneaded |

kneel | kneels | kneeling | kneeled |

knit | knits | knitting | knitted |

knock| knocks | knocking | knocked |

know | knows | knowing | knew| known |

L

lack | lacks| lacking | lacked |
last | lasts | lasting |lasted |
laugh | laughs | laughing | laughter |
lead | leads | leading | led |
learn | learns | learning | learned|
leave | leaves | leaving |leaved |
lie | lies | lying | lied |
like | likes | liking | liked |
look | looks | looking | looked |
love | loves | loving | loved |

M

maintain | maintains | maintaining | maintained |
make | makes | making | made |
manage | manages| managing | managed |
mark | marks | marking | marked |
marry | marries | marrying | married |
match | matches | matching | matched |
memorize | memorizes | memorizing | memorized |
modify | modifies | modifying | modified |
move | moves | moving | moved |
multiply | multiplies | multiplying | multiplied |

N

name | names | naming | named |
necessitate | necessitates | necessitate | necessitated |
need | needs | needing | needed |

neglect | neglects | neglecting | neglected |

negotiate | negotiates | negotiating | negotiated |

nest | nests | nesting | nested |

note | notes | noting | noted |

notice | notices | noticing | noticed |

notice | notifies | notifying | notified |

number | numbers | numbering | numbered |

O

obey | obeys | obeying | obeyed |

observe | observes | observing | observed |

obtain | obtains | obtaining | obtained |

occur | occurs | occurring | occurred |

offend | offends | offending | offended |

offer | offers | offering | offered |

omit | omits | omitting | omits |

order | orders | ordering | ordered |

overflow | overflows | overflowing | overflowed |

owe | owes | owing | owed |

P

pack | packs | packing | packed |

plant | plants | planting | planted |

please | pleases | pleasing | pleased |

pray | prays | praying | prayed |

prepare | prepares | preparing | prepared |

print | prints | printing | printed |

produce | produces | producing | produced |

promise | promises | promising | promised |

protect | protects | protecting | protected |

provides | provides | providing | provided |

Q

question | questions | questioning | questioned |

quiet | quiets | quieting | quieted |

quit | quits | quitting | quitting |

quote | quotes | quoting | quoted |

R

receive | receives | receiving | received |

refuse | refuses | refusing | refused |

regret | regrets | regretting | regretted |

remind | reminds | reminding | reminded |

reply | replies | replying | replied |

request | requests | requesting | requested |

respect | respects | respecting | respected |

return | returns | returning | returned |

review | reviews | reviewing | reviewed |

revise | revises | revising | revised |

S

satisfy | satisfies | satisfying | satisfied |

save | saves | saving | saved |

silence | silences | silencing | silent |

sit | sits | sitting | seated |

slow | slows | slowing | slowed |

smile | smiles | smiling | smiled |

spell | spells | spelling | spelled |

stop | stops | stopping | stopped |

surround | surrounds | surrounding | surrounded |

suspend | suspends | suspending | suspended |

T

talk | talks | talking | talked |

test | tests | testing | tested |

time | times | timing | timed |

touch | touches | touching | touched |

trade | trades | trading | traded |

transport | transports | transporting | transported |

trap | traps | trapping | trapped |

travel | travels | traveling | traveled |

trouble | troubles | troubling | troubled |

trust | trusts | trusting | trusted |

U

uncover | uncovers | uncovering | uncovered |

underscore | underscores | underscoring | underscored |

unfasten | unfastens | unfastening | unfastened |

unfold | unfolds | unfolding | unfolded |

unify | unifies | unification | unified |

unite | unites | uniting | united |

unload | unloads | unloading | unloaded |

unlock | unlocks | unlocking | unlocked |

unpack | unpacks | unpacking | unpacked |

use | uses | using | used |

V

vacation | vacations | vacationing | vacationed |

vacuum | vacuums | vacuuming | vacuumed |

value | values | valuing | valued |

vanish | vanishes | vanishing | vanished |

vaporize | vaporizes | vaporizing | vaporized |

vary | varies | varying | varied |

venture | ventures | venturing | ventured |

verbalize | verbalizes | verbalizing | verbalized |

visit | visits | visiting | visited |

W

wail | wails | wailing | wailed |

wait | waits | waiting | waited |

walk | walks | walking | walked |

want | wants | wanting | wanted |

warm | warms | warming | warmed |

welcome | welcomes | welcoming | welcomed |

whisper | whispers | whispering | whispered |

whistle | whistles | whistling | whistled |

wonder | wonders | wondering | wondered |

work | works | working | worked |

Now, we've come to the last and final page of your grammar book. Feel free to practice writing in small paragraphs—use the verbs and all the examples given to you in each lesson. Practice your speaking skill in English with someone you know who can help you enhance your progress. Meet with like-minded English learners weekly to practice your English communication power. Do not speak your native language during these meetings—your mind needs time to absorb what you've learned so that you will remember them well and become proficient.

Happy trails . . .

www.ingramcontent.com/pod-product-compliance
Lightning Source LLC
Chambersburg PA
CBHW080438230426
43662CB00015B/2305